" This is the book that will UNjack your car, UNburgle your home, UNabduct your child, and protect your Identity. This is the book you can't live without---because without this book, you may not live."

CONQUER *CRIME*

How To Be Your Own Bodyguard

Don Paul

A.M.D.G.

Imagine a society in which every individual denied his own interests to provide a better life for his neighbor. Each wanted the other to have the best of every business dealing. Rather than commit crimes against neighbors, each person looked out for the benefit and betterment of all those around him. Women were honored always. Sex was the medium through which true, heartfelt and forever faithful love was communicated to only one special life partner.

That society existed during America's early years when we were really one nation, under God. I wish you could now be over 200 years old so you could have been born then---in those great days when crime was the rare exception.

Prayer: "Lord, I'm aware that crime grows as we turn our backs on God. May the knowledge I offer in this book confirm what You offer in <u>Your Book</u>, The Bible. May those who read us stand with us---grateful for Your peace---that truly surpasses all understanding. Amen."

DEDICATION: To my wife.

Durch das ganze Leben ist ein Mann glueklich wenn er seine treue Liebe gefunden hat. Und meine wird fuer eine Ewigkeit in meinen Herzen sein. Genau wie Die Mutter meiner Frau gesagt hat,

"<u>MEINE CHRISTA!</u>"

Library of Congress Catalog Card Number: 96-67885

Publisher's Cataloging in Publication

Paul, Don, 1937-

Conquer Crime---Be Your Own Bodyguard. New anti-crime tricks, Identity Theft, Carjacking, Anti-child abduction, Rape protection / by Don Paul

p. cm.

Includes index

ISBN 0-938263-22-9

1. Survival. 2. Identity theft. 3. Anti-burlglary . I. Paul, Don, 1937- II. Title

TS534.5.P38 2000

623.4 '42
QB94-21211

INTRODUCING. . .
QUICK READER BOOKS by PATH FINDER

<u>New-method, how-to books.</u>

To take a productive place in society, it's a good idea to focus on one goal. In ***CONQUER CRIME*** our goal is to do what a bodyguard does for a client: **PROTECT YOUR LIFE!** The author is a former Green Beret who dug into criminal methods and created defenses to keep you safe and secure. His co-authors are several computers, so the manuscript often refers to "we" instead of "I."

Path Finder has a publishing philosophy different from others. We care about saving your time! Therefore---we use independent editors and electronic manuscript scrubbers to make sure <u>this book contains:</u>

1. Special text for speed readers
2. Easy to understand concepts
3. Crystal clear wording,

Maybe the text is choppy, but <u>I'm sure you'll understand it easily and fast.</u> My electronic scrubbers report:

> At the sub-vocalization reading rate of less than 600 wpm, you should complete this whole book in 1 hour, 55 minutes, not including box additions, which provide mental refreshment. After scrubbing, we achieved reading-ease parity with Hemingway's short stories. We average under 1.6 syllables per word. Our average sentence: Less than 15 words. Our illustrations make text and concepts easy to understand. . Finally, paragraph headings enable you to scan each chapter for the information of interest to you. I also included an index and a glossary.

Path Finder has been successful for the last 20 years because we go beyond any other knowledge in a given field and explain in simple, easy-to-understand detail, the new methods we've discovered. I interview elite military, Special Forces, Seals and PJ's, then translate that information into easy speak.

The first method we discovered was a way to keep you from getting lost without using a map. *NEVER GET LOST---THE GREEN BERET'S COMPASS COURSE* which allows you to go anywhere without a map and return to your starting point **without having to back-track.** Over 25,000 copies are in print. It's now in video*.

After that, we added to our book list and widened our distribution. We published:

Everybody's Outdoor Survival Guide
Great Livin' in Grubby Times best selling survival book.
Everybody's Knife Bible over 30,000 copies!
24 + Ways to Use Your Hammock in the Field.
How to Write a Book in 53 Days.
Shooting Forever, about handgun use and
Ammo Forever, about rifles and shotguns.
NEVER GET LOST, Video. Go anywhere, always return.
The Green Beret's Compass Course

Now comes the complete rewrite of *CONQUER CRIME.* I speak several languages, which made it easier to gather information from the gangs. As a Green Beret, I have lots of experience in planning defenses, which is probably the reason I'm still alive.

CONQUER CRIME, is a book **you can't live without because without this book, you might not live!** Surviving a criminal attack takes two critical skills. You need to be your own bodyguard------always alert to danger and capable of handling it. Also, you need a tactical outlook to conduct your life safely in many of our crime-infested jungles.

SEE OUR WEB:
www.survival-books.com   Write author: pathfindr@gte.net
(See the order coupons in the back of this book.)

HEY! If you already own a copy of *SECURE FROM CRIME,* tear out the index and we'll return a new book for half price. Maybe add a buck for postage; we'll pay the rest. (God Bless...)

CONQUER CRIME !

How To Be Your Own Bodyguard

CONTENTS

INTRODUCTION "Protect" is a process that occurs before a crime takes place. Cops don't protect; they take reports after you become a victim, then apprehend a suspect. "Protect" is something you have to do before a crime occurs, or during an attempt. Learn what to protect by discovering criminal methods and the defenses for each kind of attack.

1. PROTECTING YOUR PERSONAL SELVES Anticipate; then plan. I anticipated for you because I interviewed the criminals. Where are you vulnerable? Just as you get in and out of your car + several others. A new defense condition (DEF-CON) system keeps you safe by teaching you each defensive moves as danger gets closer. How to use pepper gas plus other grab 'n go weapons. Mental and physical training. Martial Arts? No! Firearms? Maybe.   **7**

2. SAVING YOUR IDENTITY There are two of you. One breathes, the other exists as a social security number, date of birth, address, etc. Protecting the second you is also important. Learn here how to go underground and keep your personal information all to yourself.   **19**

3. PROTECTING YOUR CASTLE Fortifying your home better than King Arthur's Castle. All about warning devices, alarm systems, hiding places and vaults you can build. How to make one special room a well-fortified sanctuary for your family's protection.   **31**

4. VEHICLE SECURITY, PARKED AND DRIVING How to avoid losing your car while driving it. Stoplight defenses, gas station surveillance, and the four right-turn method to avoid being attacked in your driveway. Things not to keep in your car. Methods of concealment. Window tinting. Car alarms? Which vehicles are more safe than others.   **45**

5. DEFENSIVE WEAPONRY How to prevail in conflicts you can't avoid. Use of non-shooting weapons to increase and strengthen your sphere of defense. Weapons all around you. Things in the home to be used for defense..   **59**

6. CRIMES AGAINST SINGLES In a severe emotional encounter, they cheat on you, steal from you, and sometimes leave you with a disease. How to check up on dates and identify predators. Special defense measures for those who are alone in the world.   **69**

7. FOR THE WEALTHY: EXTRA PRECAUTIONS Few people who acquire wealth think about increased danger of being victimized because the focus of their lives is on success, not protection. Special earnings require special care. Wealth dictates precaution. Low profiling.

8. SAFETY IN TRAVEL Your vacation can be a disaster. Choose a crime free destination. Watching out for theft. Protecting your money. Tips for traveling on foot and in public transportation. Avoiding hotel intrusions. Taxi smarts---where to sit for tactical purposes. Security measures when alone on beaches.

9. RAPE The nature of the crime: Power and control. Taking the initiative and avoiding the crime. Identifying the problem: Thieves work in pairs, rapists work alone. Using suspect proximity as a guide to positive action. Places not to be. Weapons for defense---in the home & outside.

10. AFTER THE ATTACK. Many who are intended victims win the conflict by neutralizing the attacker. If you ever fall into this category, be careful; you may be charged with a crime for winning.

11 TEENS Terrible teens make this a terrible time to be one. Parents don't pay attention, snoop dog is your friends favorite (music?) people in school want to rob you, you have to pierce your (whatever) in an attempt to be popular. Crime abounds. Life sucks.

12. CONQUERING CHILD ABDUCTION It makes me mad that all these benefit-your-child organizations can't come up with a better idea than fingerprints and pictures on milk cartons. The best idea is to recover children right away. The quick child recovery system. Train your child for night escape. Escape and Evasion is fun; here's how.

13. DATE RAPES. How to avoid. Setting test boundaries to see if your beau passes the test or tries to pass the boundaries. Lectures on alcohol and the date rape drugs they may contain.

14. FIREARMS Bringing conflict to the level of lethal. Choosing gun first is a bad idea. Choose ammo you can shoot. Then buy the tool that makes it move. The wonderful world of shot for defense. Sizes and ways to shoot from a completely secure position.

CONQUER CRIME

Be Your Own Bodyguard

by
Don Paul

INTRODUCTION

"Fail to prepare, and you prepare to fail."

Twenty thousand copies ago I wrote a book about defending yourself from crime. I was living in California at that time, so I accepted speaking engagements. I began with a question: "How many here would like to be eligible for police protection?" Everyone raised a hand. I continued, "Now let me tell you a fact. Police can only make an arrest AFTER a crime has been committed. Therefore, if you want to be eligible for police protection, you first have to become a victim. Now how many...?"

WANT TO HAVE DINNER WITH A CONVICT?

In California right now, approximately 83,000 convicted felons are free because the courts decided that overcrowding in prisons was cruel and unusual punishment. (Apparently, no constitutional issue of felons overcrowding our society was considered.)

If you want to interview a rapist or a burglar, call a bail bondsman or probation officer and ask for help in setting up a dinner. Booze brings out revelations.

Since I first wrote, many new ways of stealing, robbing and assaulting you have become popular. Formerly you had most to worry about protecting yourself, your family and your property. Today, more is at stake. Unthinkable in earlier years, we now witness the theft of a person's complete identity. (See chapter 2)

We're being told the crime rate has gone down. Do you think the classification of crimes has been changed by justice to produce a better image for the current administration?

Why is crime almost always the number one story on every news cast? It's as if the news is the same every night---only the names of the victims and perpetrators change. We build a prison per week in this country. I interviewed a prison administrator from California who told me they completed 23 new prisons in the late 90's and are still overcrowded.

COULD THE CRIME RATE EXPLODE SOON?

What factors could cause a huge loss of effective criminal containment? What if a war caused a manpower drain and left us only with those disqualified for military service---such as convicts? Can our different races blacks, browns, Asians and whites coexist in peace? What about unequal economic status between neighbors (generally poor robs rich; rich cheats poor)? Most important---twenty years ago, government welfare caused a new generation of babies without fathers and today many of those kids are gang bangers. Are we at risk?

Early Americans shared a common set of values. That's no longer the case. Various colors and sub-cultures steal from and brutalize everyone. Drugs eradicate any remaining shred of fear or dread of consequence in a criminal who wants to attack you or your family. Your property, your body, or your life mean nothing. Gang people surround themselves with a subculture full of resentment and bitterness. Rebellion against the law is heroic.

Do you really have to prepare now? Witness the L.A. riots after Rodney King. As the riots began, the police retreated. The National Guard showed up---without ammunition. Mayor Bradley and Jesse Jackson spoke out apologetically about the poor rioters.

2

Good citizens couldn't purchase guns or ammunition to defend themselves against criminals who were already armed.

THIS BOOK WILL PREPARE YOU . . .

You can survive against those who will turn outlaw under a variety of circumstances. This is how I went about writing: First, I needed to find out how the bad guys are plying their trades. Speaking fluent Spanish helped me interview gang members and other individuals who specialize in crime. Many former gang members who are now converts to Christianity have been extremely helpful. I studied how criminals think and therefore learned how to predict a lot of their actions. I discovered not only how the germ operates, but also why. With that information, I used my military and police background to formulate defenses. This book prepares you to protect:

1. Your person and your loved ones.
2. Your property.
3. Your identity.

Incidentally, learn this now:

Don't risk #1 to save #2 or #3.

After I wrote the original version of this book, I was invited to appear on over 250 media shows. Radio and TV show hosts liked me because I had original ideas about crime prevention. The format of the shows went something like this:

INTRODUCTION, "Don Paul, former Green Beret, cop, wrote six other books on survival, etc."

QUESTIONS BY HOST AND CONVERSATION. "I read your book and I want to know---."

HOST OPENS LINES TO CALLERS. The variety of callers and questions amazed me. The range was from a blind lady in Canada who was terrified to a landlord who promised to shoot any intruder with his new .44 magnum. On a TV show in Sacramento, a scared kid about 13 years old wanted to know what gun I recommended that he carry to school. Hundreds of questions during hundreds of hours proved that people were eager to learn how to protect themselves---because police can't.

3

> Situation: I was patrol cop in Linda Vista, San Diego. Old man, 72 owned a Nash Rambler station wagon from which thieves stole battery. He installed an auto alarm. It sounded off at 0200 A.M. He saw battery thief in progress. He grabbed his cane and ran to protect his property. Perp said, "Old man, get outta my face. Can't you see I'm busy stealing this battery." Old man began to beat on thief with cane, who laughed at him. Old man had heart attack and died.
>
> I arrived in time to console a grief stricken widow and take a report on a stolen battery. Incidentally, San Diego's then district attorney would have prosecuted the old man if he had shot the perp with a gun. In many States, you're not allowed to use lethal force to protect property.

Protect is something one does <u>before</u> a crime occurs or <u>during</u> its commission. The law is clear on this: **Police can make an arrest only AFTER a crime has been committed**.

So <u>protection is a do-it-yourself proposition</u>. After you become a victim, the police will take a report. To keep your home, your person and your loved ones safe from crime, you first have to learn how the bad guys operate, and then set security measures in place. You need to develop a personal defense plan for yourself and your home. If you want to *win during* the inevitable battle, you'll have to prepare before the battle begins. That's what this book teaches you.

I appeared on G. Gordon Liddy's talk show after he had written an article for *Forbes Magazine* titled, *SECURITY.* It reads:

> "There are essentially two kinds of people in this world, and they can be distinguished easily by their reaction to life-threatening situations such as the invasion of one's home. All resort to prayer. But it is by the text of their prayers ye shall know them. For some it's a version of `God, please don't let them find me,' then when found, `God, please don't let them hurt me.' or, `God, please let the police get here in time!' Such persons have elected to be life's victims and, indeed, only God can help

them. There are others, however, who've chosen not to be victims. . . Their prayer. . . is for the intruder: `May God have mercy on your soul.' "

Our justice system has put limits on the cure, so the disease flourishes. If doctors worked under the same restraints as police do today, their practice would be limited because germs and viruses would have rights! No health official could kill mosquitoes until *after* they had bitten and infected you. You couldn't take antibiotics until *after* an infection had done damage.

What about criminal attitudes? Like the germ he is, he already hates you. It isn't a personal problem with you; it only appears that way. He hates, period. Witness the random violent deaths in the news. Hundreds of other victims who might not make the news because they weren't murdered are only beaten, robbed, or raped.

To a criminal's way of thinking, the act of stealing inflates self image, so they constantly search for new victims. It's a real rush to break into a house, steal a car, grab a purse and run, or kill somebody. Succeed, and their peers consider them a hero. Fail, and they get acceptance and appreciation for trying to buck the system anyway. Crime astounds many of us because we see how easy it would be to apply the same effort to honest enterprise and accumulate wealth. Why is it then that so many choose the evil way to go? They simply have to conquer, take, deceive, steal, and cheat. To a criminal, the pleasure in earning is nothing compared to the rush from making a big score after breaking the law. It elevates them.

How does most street crime take place? Against targets of opportunity. You, or your property becomes somebody's prey because attacking or stealing is convenient. Where do we face threats? Everywhere. We're at risk in our homes, in the family car, on vacation, at work and school, and anytime we're exposed

---

Allow me a definition: **Crime is like a disease. Criminals are the germs and viruses that make us all sick.**

to the public. Now the new crime, identity theft, proves you can be exposed without knowing it. People who never met you and who live thousands of miles away can target you.

To stay safe, apply the great bodyguard maxim. **"Don't get out of trouble. Keep out of trouble."**

This book teaches you to do what most good elite military forces do—-minimize your risk. You'll learn how to plan your defense, develop an anti-victim attitude, and therefore live in much improved safety and peace.

OVERSEAS PRISONS—A CHEAP DETERRENT

I recently interviewed a man who worked in Sacramento for the Bureau of Corrections. In the past, some 84,000 convicted felons roamed in California, let out of prisons because they were overcrowded. To solve the problem, California recently built 23 new prisons. Even with the new construction, thousands more prisoners have to be freed and the State is again crawling with convicts.

***

Especially when early releases are flooding society with human sewage before treatment, where does it say that after committing a crime, the US owes a criminal a free ride in an American prison?

I wonder what it would do to the crime problem if a criminal knew in advance that conviction would secure him a vacation at a nice crossbar hotel, in say, Turkey?

Solution: Contract with foreign governments in Third World countries to take care of our prisoners on a lease basis. We can lease prison facilities in South Korea or Mexico for a fraction of what it cost here at home. Problems with visitation? Establish a tele-communications network. Prisoners could view their loved ones via TV and vice versa.

Chapter 1

PERSONAL DEFENSE MEASURES

If you ever study the job of body guarding, you'll learn: Dead clients don't write checks. What's the best way to keep your check-writing client alive? Anticipate; then plan. Look for trouble, then avoid it. Remember Ben Franklin's advice: *A stitch in time saves nine.* The title of this book is *CONQUER CRIME;* **not** *CONQUER CRIMINALS.* It's a lot easier to **avoid** a criminal than it is to defeat one in combat. Anytime you have to pull your weapon, fight off an attacker or run for your life to get away, you probably made a body guarding error. Most victims wind up in their condition for one of two reasons. B. They let their guard down and thought they were safe. A. They made no preparations.

If you don't prepare---you won't be aware. So it's important that you take precautions---as many as you can. You don't have to break your bones in a Karate class. As a matter of fact, I don't recommend Karate because it draws you into combat situations you could lose. My own Karate instructor told his class, if you see a knife or gun, running away is your best idea.

PRINCESS DI DEAD! ACCIDENT OR ASSASSINATION?
When I heard the news, I was heartbroken---then angry. Being her bodyguard would have been extremely difficult because she was rich, famous, and had mortal enemies. Also, precautions have to increase when the protectee is rich and famous. She was more popular than her royal husband---and therefore had become a royal pain. Now we learn that taps existed on telephones of her personal friends to provide tracking and future travel information. Would the English Crown perhaps be annoyed by her impending marriage to Dodi so that the new step father of the Crown Prince's children would be Muslim? Would that disturb the Royals? Knowing the situation, wouldn't the bodyguard be alerted enough to step up precautions?

Was someone buying drinks in the bar for the driver or was alcohol added to his blood after the accident?

Was a high speed chase a normal occurrence when the papparrazi knew where she was going? How simple would it be to implant a front tire with a small explosive pellet that would explode from centrifugal force and blow that tire at high speed? Was the car left unguarded so that anyone could have deflated a tire, dropped the tiny explosive in through a tire stem and re-inflated?

Today, many areas of the United States are much like Vietnam during the war. We own it during the day, but the night belongs to criminals. Many people stay at home after dark, which is one reason Internet shopping is popular. Still, you would be amazed at the number of attacks on "ordinary, honest citizens" that occur in places you'd think a sensible person would avoid.

You can learn from their mistakes. Near convenience stores, rape, assault and battery occur frequently. In addition, the 24 hour Auto-Tellers are dangerous to use after dark. When I first wrote this book, I subscribed to a service which gathered facts on ATM robberies. One guy stole a skip loader from a rental yard at 0200 A. M. and drove it to the ATM. He was apprehended driving down a street with the whole ATM machine in the skip loader bucket! People who steal money from you at any ATM during the night are just as desperate. Moreover, they're probably high on a drug. Think about that desperation and consider the possibilities.

A perp with a knife hides in the bushes out near where the cars park for ATM patrons. While you're in the light, you lose your night vision. The perp can move about in the dark unobserved. On defense: Sweep the area with a spotlight, or at least headlights before stopping. Lock your car to avoid having the perp climb in and hide. You might be attacked as you return to your car. On defense: Carry a visible weapon, ready to use.

Other areas are dangerous, too. Be particularly cautious in community parks, amusement parks, poorly lit streets, X-rated movie areas, red light districts, hangouts for drug peddlers, areas with a vagrant populace (like beach parking lots), and areas with a high concentration of derelict buildings. Any one of these places could well be the last you visit.

Hospitals are now hazardous to your health in one specific area—parking lots. After dark, weirdos just love the target-rich environment offered by shift-changing nurses. The thugs 'n drugs crowd like to pick on doctors and their vehicles. Visit hospitals during the early afternoon hours whenever possible. If you have to visit after dark, carry a weapon (ready to use).

WATCH OUT IN ELEVATORS

Your health and safety dictate: Use the stairs. Older public elevators are dangerous. If you step into one from the lobby and select an upper floor, it may still go down to answer the call of the thief or pervert lurking in the basement or underground parking.

Solution: Step in by yourself from the lobby. Push, B, L, and 5 (Basement Lobby, and any upper floor), then step back out into the lobby. On the elevator location indicator on top of the main doors, watch it go down to the basement and come back up. When it stops at the lobby empty the second time, climb aboard to go up. If your elevator stops before you get where you're going and a suspicious thug gets in, step off. Stand near the operating panel in case you need help. As soon as the perp leaves after a purse snatch, hit the alarm button. It makes him run so witnesses know whom to identify.

ARMED MUGGING—THE MORE PERSONAL TOUCH

IF YOU'RE A ROBBERY VICTIM

Cooperate. Nothing you own is worth what it will cost to fix your body if you panic, which in turn will cause the robber to panic. Stay cool. Chances are good you won't be shot. Use your time to discover who your assailant is.

Since attending the FBI academy in San Diego, I can tell you the height and weight of just about anybody. Not you though---and don't try. How tall? Top of head matched this stationary object (in a super market, (the vegetable soup?) How heavy. Normally skinny. Any bigger than average muscles?

What did the guy smell like? Not his after shave, but bad breath and body odor indicate how scared **he** was. If scared, then new to the trade, and police won't waste time looking for old pros.

How is this guy dressed? Not the color of clothes, but the class. If tattered, this is a guy down on his luck.

Even if you don't know guns, notice the hole at the end of the barrel. Quarter inch? Cheap gun. Half inch, scary gun. Could you see the bullets in the revolving cylinder? If not, probably automatic.

How old? Try to peg it exactly. Even without checking his appearance, listen to his voice and you will get a good idea. Any expressions you remember? Cool.

Is your robber loaded on alcohol or drugs? Alcohol smells. Most inexperienced robbers have to get half loaded in order to do the act. Be careful, though. Most bullet wounds occur not because of loaded guns, but because of loaded shooters.

How did the guy leave? On foot. Into a car? Could you get the car make, license number, type, color?

Reconsider the psychological state of the mugger. He's just dropping down off a drug high. You think you had a bad day? This is the worst. So, he pulls a knife or pistol, aims it at you and says, "Give me your wallet!"

Don't respond aggressively. Don't become indignant. That makes perps horribly mad. Remember the mind of the criminal. He wants, needs to get up and over. If you disrespect

Don't carry credit cards with your money. If your credit card is in your wallet, you may get shot. Why? Because fences will pay a higher price for a stolen credit card when they know the victim is dead and can't cancel the card.

Crime report: German tourist targeted in Miami was rear ended. She got out of the car after the accident and the perps knocked her down and took her wallet. After finding credit cards there, they ran over her and she died.

him, especially in front of acquaintances, he will have to kill you in order to save face. The idea is not to die. Instead, buy life by cooperating as best you can. Be gracious and say something like: "No problem, take it all." You don't have to show fear, but you'd better show respect. That's why he bought the weapon. Make him like your attitude.

Insure your life with whatever you can give him. Make sure you have something to give—at least a $10, better a $20.

IF YOU'RE TAKEN HOSTAGE

This is a hard choice. The difference between real life and reel life (TV) have caused some deaths, I'm sure. Never allow yourself to be kidnapped. If you get shot in the city with a handgun and the bullet does not wound you in the CNS (Central Nervous System), local paramedics can keep you alive. Let some jerk take you into the hills where help is not available, and you can bleed to death from a relatively simple knife wound.

Suppose your captor uses you as a shield while shooting at someone else. Grab his gun with both your hands. Try to collapse his wrist inward so his weapon points back at him. If you continue

This happens frequently. Purse snatch victim loses all. A day later she takes a phone call form a female who says, "I just found your purse in a dumpster with your all your I.D. and credit cards in it. If you come to Denny's right away, I'll give it to you."

Victim runs out of the house and storms off in the car. Surprise! Phone call was from cellular nearby and the purse snatchers burglarized the house by using keys from purse while victim was on wild goose chase.

to twist inward, he'll have to let go. Also, if you have his weapon in both your hands while you fall to the ground, any self-respecting swat team member will have no trouble making the hostage-taker holey---via bullet placement.

RECOGNIZING TROUBLE ON THE HORIZON

Most educated people wouldn't travel in a South American jungle at night. But, as anyone with jungle experience will tell you, those jungles are much safer than our city streets. If you want to be secure from crime, you have to assess the dangers out there realistically. I can't stress this enough: **The best defense against violence is to avoid places where violence is most likely to occur.**

Can you bring a friend with you? Whether you're walking on the street or driving in any kind of vehicle, warn each other of potentially dangerous situations. If you suspect anybody, watch

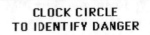
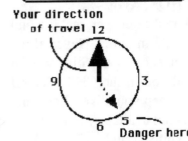

his hands. Tell your companion about your suspicions. Identify the location of the trouble so you both understand. As you travel, you move towards 12:00 o'clock, with three on your right and nine on your left. So---suppose you're being followed by a shady looking character off to your right. You say, "There's a creep following us at five o'clock 15 yards out."

WHAT CAN YOU DO ABOUT THE DANGER ?

Probably, the **DefCon** (short for **Def**ense **Con**dition) system may work best. First, assess the danger. Consider the neighborhood and your surroundings, the proximity of the suspected perpetrator, and the suspect's movement and appearance. If the guy looks weird or out of place, assume he is trouble. Many macho people show off tatoos, pierced body parts and gross looking facial hair to display rebellion. You need to decide if they're really dangerous.

You have tasks to do as soon as you sense danger—-you prepare in stages. Maybe you sense danger when you can't really see or hear anything. That's your first notice, your warning order. Size things up. How many of the enemy? Are they focused on you? Are they within 10 yards?

DEFENSE CONDITION
DISTANCE FACTORS

#1 10 yards
#2 5-6 yards
#3 3 yards
You are here

If the answer to any of the above questions indicates trouble, go to **DefCon 1**. That means get control of your weapon and get it ready. If your weapon is a handgun, then your hand is on it. Watch these people. Give this problem your full and <u>obvious</u> attention, and look for a way out.   Also check behind you for a silent partner. Choose an escape route, or at least a place that gives you a defensive advantage. Perhaps it's a crowded store you can duck into, or some men in uniform you can ask for help.

DefCon 2 occurs after you have made tactical moves to avoid the problem, and the problem persists.   It's now 5-6 yards away and closing in on you.   You're closer to an escape route. Maybe you've moved towards help. You've double-surveyed your area 360° to check for additional trouble. Your plan of defense is clear, and you're getting ready. If you carry a handgun, it may still be hidden, but the safety is off and you're prepared to fire.

At 3 yards, with things getting progressively worse, you'll have to make an offensive move. Take a stand. Get control of the situation. You can say, "Stop right there! You people are scaring me. If you want to avoid severe pain, turn around and leave right now!" This is **DefCon 3**, and the next step is shoot. Once you've issued a warning, you have a right to be afraid. Fear for your life is grounds to spray gas, attack with a non-shooting weapon, or let lead fly. When all your DefCon 3 options have been used, go to war. Win decisively. Don't wound or try to disable; shoot to kill.

Make your first shot count. Your second shot, (in the air) is your warning shot. You will be asked (perhaps in court) is you fired a warning shot. Answer: "Yes."

STAYING AWARE

Knowledge and awareness are most important for self-defense. <u>Always pay attention to what is going on.</u> When driving, listen to the news. A police scanner in your car can warn you of trouble ahead. When at home, learn to listen for telltale sounds indicating trouble. Don't turn up your television, stereo or car radio so loud that it blocks out other sounds. A squeaky door, floorboards creaking, or the sound of broken glass should alert you. Head phones make you deaf to your surroundings. You must be able to hear; not be heard.

Learn a trick from karate instructors: Don't stare ahead at one point; soften your focus. Train yourself to see everything 180° in front of you. Look away from bright light sources, or wear glasses and use window shades or drapes to help you. When you look into the sun outdoors or into bright lights indoors, you're at a disadvantage. You must be able to see; not to be seen.

Besides being cautious, show restraint in dress. Don't display wealth or expensive jewelry. Wear gloves over your rings until you're in friendly surroundings. Parking lot attendants, cab drivers, or ticket takers at the opera often pass on information for extra cash.

Develop a low profile. Two editions ago when I first wrote this book, it may have been enough to tell you not to buy season tickets to the opera or ball game in your name or have any tickets sent to your home address because the list of season ticket holders could be pilfered and used by burglars. Now, things are worse and computers have enabled criminals to make big gains with any information they get.

TOTAL SECURITY

Buy a shredder so no papers can be stolen from your trash. If you list your phone number, list it with a nickname or use the name of the family pet. Then if a phone caller asks for your pet, let him sell something to your dog. Utility bills can be mailed to any name you care to use if you make a security deposit. Just list your utility account number on the checks you use for payment.

Your home address should appear on none of your personal identification. Get a privately owned mail box (Mail Boxes Etc.) or at least a post office box address for your driver's license and vehicle registration. If it isn't that way now, fill out a form and change it. Thus, whoever steals your wallet doesn't get your home address. Use the same mailing address on your other belongings. If you must have a mailing address on your key ring, use a friend's. That way, keys found by Samaritans return to you. Stolen keys by burglars send them to the wrong residence. Likewise, use your mail box address on baggage labels at airports. Why? Baggage handlers have been known to sell information to house burglars---who would just love to know you'll be gone for a few weeks.

More and more, people shop by phone with a credit card across state lines to avoid state sales taxes. (Some states collect no sales tax on out-of-state deliveries.) Never give your home address to any stranger, especially over the phone. Take delivery at your mail box address (which is the same place to which your credit card bill is mailed).

PHONE SECURITY

In conversation with friends, use an, " I'm OK" code message. For example, "Buddy's doing fine," means: Everything's all right. Without that being said over the phone, it means, "I'm in trouble and I need help right away." That way, you send a trouble message no criminal would understand.

VARY YOUR ACTIVITY

Don't establish patterns of travel and activity. Interested thieves keep notes on your arrival and departures. Don't drive the same route every day; take as many different routes as possible to work and school. Leave and return at different times. Computers and modems are creating new home employment opportunities. Any time you can work at home instead of the office, you decrease your exposure.

> **BANKS WITH BULLET PROOF GLASS PROTECTING TELLERS**
> You can use these, but only if you bank by mail. Installed to protect against bank robbery, they've put customers at risk. Why? Several reports cite robbers who grabbed a customer, put a gun to **her** head, and demanded money.

Discussing your wealth with strangers or casual acquaintances is very poor security. Referencing your Mercedes, your summer home, or 'Daddy's little ole factory' are all poor choices for casual conversation with any but your closest friends. While we're at it, don't reserve any parking space anywhere in your own name. I recommend labeling the spaces with code names (perhaps Mickey Mouse, Goofy etc,) and rotating the names every so often. Otherwise, anybody with a pair of binoculars can find out the bosses' license numbers, trace the car to the house, and then set up a kidnap or robbery.

Engrave everything you own. Thieves have been known to leave engraved goods alone because fences pay less for engraved property. Also, police catch thieves and recover thousands in stolen goods. If engraved, you get them back and the prosecution's case is stronger. If not, no evidence; the perps go free and your possessions go to a police auction.

Trust nobody. Today, many police departments hire bad apples partially because Federal laws have compelled them to lower standards. Also, with all the drug money around, temptation is tremendous. In Kailua, Oahu, Hawaii, the police department discovered several officers connected with burglars and stolen property. Some resigned, and the newspapers never published the names of others. In San Diego, an attorney who was president of the local Bar Association was indicted for receiving stolen property. He apparently was fencing for several thieves, many of whom were his clients.

Never give any stranger your complete key ring. Make sure the valet parking is real. It's far better to arrange to park the car yourself and keep your keys. House keys left in trust with your neighbor get no ID tag because an enterprising thief or teenage guest next door can pocket your key for future use.

DAYTIME BURGLARY, OWNER DECOYED

With house doors locked, keep a cordless phone with you on your property. Many burglars enter homes by day when owners are busy outside. Others steal from occupied homes during TV shows at night. Their trick: Timing. Never be in the house during commercials. Steal quick.

An open front door into your house may draw you in to a burglary in progress, and a high percentage of these become violent. Call police. Let them clear the house.

HOW POLICE FUNCTION---MOST OF THE TIME

They take reports—*after*. That's especially true because of the Rodney King incident. What wife would encourage her law enforcement husband to confront a criminal? If the criminal wins, she attends a tragic funeral and gets a flag. If the officer wins, the criminal's relatives will file a lawsuit and the officer may be suspended, lose his job, or be taken away from his family to go to prison.

Also, in many areas, county sheriffs and city police don't cooperate. Even though you live in the city, police won't take a report on a theft you think occurred in the county. Sheriffs' crime reports often don't filter to police. That's because some sheriffs don't want police to solve crimes. City police chiefs also want their statistics high, which doesn't happen when sheriffs apprehend criminals from the city. Political infighting and bitterness between elected officials puts citizens more at risk.

THIS HAPPENED. Citizen who lived near county line was burglarized. Calls sheriffs. "Where do you live? Oh, that's in the city, call police."

Police took report.

Sheriff's deputy discovers stolen material, but does nothing because no report was forwarded to sheriff.

Result: Thieves loot in the city, transport a few blocks to county and stay relatively safe from discovery.

Shoulder surfing is one of the latest "victimless" crimes. Say you make a credit card call from an airport. Any one of several well-rewarded spotters will look over your shoulder to copy the number, which is sold immediately to pay phone calling stations all over the country. Then the number is re-sold---mostly to callers from South of the border who run up an unbelievable bill on your credit card!

The *before* and *during* time frames of a crime are up to you. Almost always, the police handle the *after* when they write up the report. The steps you take *before* a crime happens may make the difference between your living unmolested or becoming a victim. Use the time you have *before* to plan what will happen *during*. Once you formulate your plan and practice, your life should go along smoothly with little interference from the criminal germs and viruses all around you.

WOMEN. If you purchase a handgun, purchase one with less than a six inch barrel. Long barrels make it easy for a criminal invader to grab a gun away from a defender. See chapter 14.

Reference: Paxton Quiqley's *ARMED AND FEMALE*. plus *NOT AN EASY TAREGET*. She (Paxton) and I appeared together as co-guests with Michael Jackson hosting for KABC. She knows what she is talking about.

This person
YOU
could be
attacked.

THE REAL,
PERSONABLE,
PHYSICAL, HUMAN
YOU

This person
YOUR IDENTITY
could be
stolen
and disgraced.

THE IMPERSONAL,
SOCIAL SECURITY
NUMBERED, DOB'd,
ADDRESSED, PHONE
NUMBERED AND
UTILITY USING
YOU

Chapter 2

STOLEN IDENTITY

You're not OK when somebody else becomes you.

If you are working, pay bills on time, this information applies. It used to be, the person on the left in the illustration was all you had to worry about. To rob that person, someone had to locate you and then use force or stealth to take away your belongings. Insurance might reimburse you.

As you well know, there is another you---your identity. People who steal your identity reap far more than burglars or thieves. Penalties for this crime are not severe. When profits are high and risk is low, any crime will become popular.

In this chapter, we focus on the guy or gal on the right side of the opening illustration: YOUR IDENTITY. After the crimes occur, you can learn about what to do---pay $40 for a book that teaches recovery. But I'm your bodyguard so I'll protect you--- which is something that takes place **before** the crime occurs. Let's decide to protect all of "your personal identifying information." I want to shield your identity so well that not even big brother can find you. This is what we have to keep from exposure:

Your name.
YOUR SOCIAL SECURITY NUMBER
Your residential *and business* address.
Your phone numbers
Your driver's license number
Your place of employment.
Your employee identification number
Your mother's maiden name
Your bank account numbers
Your credit card numbers

We'll deal with all of these but first, let's discuss the nature of the crime and how it might affect you.

Imagine this: You work all your life to pay your bills and maintain a good credit rating. You have dignity, self respect, and pride in all the financial security your life's work has enabled you to acquire. Then one day you apply for credit. It's denied. You're astounded. You write for a credit report and discover that you're over $50,000 in debt and several months delinquent in payment. No bank will loan you a nickel. You've bounced checks.

---
*They open a new credit card account in your name. HOW COULD THIS HAPPEN! This really peeves me because it would be simple for the credit card companies to digitize voice patterns and obtain a visual match when you called. Why not? Too expensive?

How did all this happen? Criminals have "borrowed" your name, social security number and date of birth as if it were a car. Then they took your name on a joy ride, had several crashes, then took it to a chop shop and stripped it of the last ounce of value. You're disgraced---and economically damaged.

Called "IDENTITY THEFT," it occurs when someone else collects your vital information and uses it to act as if he were you. It's sort of like cloning. Only instead of creating another hard working, honest you, they create a non-working bad you with your credit rating, new credit cards, your checks from an account they opened in your name, and your ability to buy whatever they want as if they **were** you.

Guess what? In 1995 the total amount lost to identity thieves was 442 million. In 1997, that amount jumped to 745 million. In my latest phone conversation with the Secret Service, they report still a further increase in this crime's popularity.

HOW DID YOU BECOME SO VULNERABLE?

Greed and the hunger for power and control always create a ripple effect in society. Scripture says, "The love of money is the root of all evil." Maybe the Writer knew what He was talking about. If one price gouges, others are sure to follow. When a majority in society want to get rich quick, inflation follows along to destroy an economy. In this case, information brokers simply wanted to gather and sell information about everybody for profit. Criminals get easy access to the information and steal identities on a regular basis.

Also, your government has invaded your privacy far beyond what many might think reasonable. One example: Eaves dropping on private conversations all over the world (reported on *60 MINUTES* see additional box below) as well as illegal wiretaps.

What does the government do with information it gathers on you? Sells---to anybody. One example: Motor vehicle departments make frequent sales to the public.

Not only could this happen to you now, but the latest happens after you go to Judgement. Somebody reads your obituary and goes to county records for a death certificate, which lists your vital information. Bingo. They apply for credit cards, open a new account at a bank and the new "you" gets to go on living in the evil mode. If nobody notifies the three major credit reporting agencies of your death, applications continue. Is there a defense? Yes, but after you pass on to Eternity, only your executor can defend.

First, let's figure out the many ways someone might attack. Then we'll set up defenses and traps.

WILL THEY CHOOSE YOU TO BE A VICTIM?

Many police agencies treat identity theft as a victimless crime. When someone buys a lot of goods with your credit card, opens up a phony bank account in your name, or incurs a ton of debt you're supposed to pay for, you're not financially burdened too much, and your credit can be restored. Enforcement is lax because plenty of other crimes take precedence. Ask any detective about his case load. Homicides and robberies certainly take precedence over a crime where only a credit card company loses.

The big deal to the victim is this: Loss of credit privileges until the matter can be cleared up. In a few instances, the victims have been falsely arrested for crimes committed by their impersonators.

> This happened: Woman identity thief sought out look-alike victim from published photos. After maxing out a credit card, she bought jewelry with a bad check written in victim's name. Later while under oath in court, the store owner later identified the victim as the person who wrote the check . That was an easy mistake for the store owner to make since the victim was first chosen because of her look-alike semblance to the real criminal. Trouble city!

HOW THIEVES STEAL YOUR DATA

They get your photograph from a business card, published newsletter, or perhaps a yearbook.

They steal mail out of your residential mailbox and obtain your credit card bill. (Is the flag on your mail box up to signal outgoing mail so thieves can easily plunder?) Then they'll call the credit card company and ask that the bill be sent to your new address_____. You don't get the bill for a couple of months or so until you call and ask. Wow! Do you owe them some money or what?

Other ways to get your information include: Steal wallet or purse with SS# inside. Steal plastic bags full of papers & personal data from your trash. (Use a shredder). From the post office, they fill out a form that says you moved. So now all your mail comes to the new address, which is a commercial box number

(MAIL BOX USA). If they time it just before you go on vacation, then you won't miss your mail while they gather your information.

They can use www.docusearch.com, or a variety of other information brokers. Of course, the information costs money, but the gangs don't care. Once they have put together enough information from one victim, they can charge others' information to the original victim's credit card over the phone or internet.

Business cards are routinely sent by firms in the mail when asked this question: "Could you send me some information on the (products, real estate or services you have to sell) along with the name of a contact person? As soon as the card arrives, credit agencies will give the identity thief the key piece of data he needs: Your Social Security #.

They get personal information from your files at work. (Night janitorial services?) Also on the increase: **They surf and sift the internet.** They get your secrets from an unscrupulous information broker who has built a large data base from all of the above sources.

Of all the ways in which to acquire enough information about you to steal your identity, this is most common: **They get your credit report.** Now, selling your credit report to just anybody violates the law. So the credit reporting agencies get around the law by releasing only "header" information---which contains your name, address, etc., plus your social security number! Once thieves have that piece of information, they can target you.

Show on *60 Minutes* discussed US ability to listen to <u>every</u> phone call and most private conversations occurring in U.S. and all over the world.

Reported: Lady in East was asked by friend over phone how her son performed in the school play. She answered, "He bombed." An investigation opened by Feds because "bombed" is a word tagged by voice recognition software.

OPERATION <u>SPEND IT ALL!</u>

Various identity thieves have different motives. Some want a better life, more prestige, more respect. Others want to get

24

away from a vengeful ex spouse. Still others want just a little extra spending cash or perhaps the ability to charge a 1-900 phone call to your credit card without getting caught by a wife who sees the phone bill. This chapter is not about those people.

This chapter is about organized crime guys who want big money from lots of different identities---one of them yours. This is their primary job and they do it well.

YOUR BEST DEFENSE . . .

. . .is a good offense. Make all your critical data top secret. Don't wait till someone steals your identity and <u>then</u> try to recover. You not only have to <u>call</u> credit agencies to set the record straight, but you have to <u>write</u> them and include proof. In my opinion, that's a small effort compared to the cost of recovery.

DIRECT MARKETING ASSOCIATION
<u>Mail preference service</u>
Box 9008
Farmingdale, NY. 11735

DIRECT MARKETING ASSOCIATION
<u>Telephone preference service</u>
Box 9014
Farmingdale, N.Y. 11735

A couple of pro-active measures will cost under a dollar. Let's begin. Write to the direct marketing association and block your name from all non-locally-generated junk mail. You can get return receipt requested mail to prove they were notified, which in turn alerts them to the fact that you may be serious later on in if you have to litigate. Write to both.

Reduce your profile. Your photograph doesn't need to be in a directory of college professors, list of physicians, yellow pages, business card, or organizations employees' data board. Seeing your picture won't help the people you want to serve but it can do real damage in the hands of an **identity thief** you need to avoid.

DIRECT MARKETING ASSOCIATION
Telephone preference service
Box 9014
Farmingdale, N.Y. 11735   **DATE & TIME**
    According to my rights under the law, I hereby
instruct you to remove my name, address, phone number,
and any other data you may have on me from the lists
you sell or otherwise publish, distribute, purvey, or share.
    Please notify me by email, return mail, or phone
message that this has been accomplished.
    To ensure this happens in a timely fashion, I have
subscribed to a service which checks to verify that this
has occurred.
    If my name is still retained by your association
upon checking, then I will complain to the proper
government authorities and perhaps pursue litigation as
advised by counsel.
    Sincerely,

NAME, FULL MAILING ADDRESS AND PHONE NUMBER

Phone companies don't tell you this unless you ask, but non-published numbers and un-listed numbers are different. Unlisted means not in the directory but often available through information services AND found in reverse directories. So anybody with your phone number can locate your personal address. Non-published is better. Those numbers can't be given out by the phone company nor found in any directory. Incidentally, you only need one phone number. If you want a second one, choose a voice mail service and wear a pager. When someone dials the voice mail company, your pager goes off so you can call back.

You can put a blocker on your phones which disallows the answering party from getting your phone number when you return the call.

ALWAYS use PO Box or commercial address (MAIL BOXES, ETC.) for all sensitive mail. Use a pen-name for most commercial transactions. So, for catalogs, utility bills, non-published phone listings, create a new name.

Change the address on your auto registration to your commercial address. In the chapter on carjacking, you will see how to hide your auto registration so information could not be stolen along with your home keys or your garage opener. Here, however, we need to change the address for the record. Why? Motor vehicle departments generate extra cash by selling the lists.

WOMEN: Screen all your calls. If you live alone, ask a male friend with a deep voice to record your greeting message.

PERSONAL CHECKS

Never use personal checks for shopping. If you do, then all the information on those checks will be recorded and resold by the check clearing agencies, such as Tel-check. For some, that means your social security number, (the absolute secret you must keep). But look what they get, even if your social security number is not on the check: Street address, phone number, and of course, your bank account number, which is just about all a germ needs to begin doing damage.

Use personal checks for paying bills from home only. They need contain no personal information. They look like starter checks on a new account. For example, let's say your real name is Jon Q. Public. You've chosen a pen-name for utilities, magazine subscriptions, etc. The bill comes. You or your computer writes the check, and the signature reads Mr. Pen Name. On the lower left portion (information line) of the check, you include the item you bought or the service you received plus the payee's invoice number. Mail from a post office; not from home. Later when you

---

DO NOT return calls if you don't recognize the caller. A few germ deviants have called hundreds of pagers in the U.S. and left a call-back number. Hundreds of return callers dialed a disguised 1-900 number in Puerto Rico which later showed up on victims' billings at $2.99 per minute.

receive those cleared checks with your statement, you can prove you paid.

Keep track of your billing cycles on a calender or computer. If you don't get a bill on time, chances are it's winding up in someone else's trash.

Shred all documents before trashing them to keep dumpster divers from earning a living at your expense. Send no personal information over the internet. Those lines are insecure and just about anyone can tap into your information. The one item that is classified top secret is your social security number. Don't print it or publish it or reveal it anywhere. I've talked to several clerks representing travel agencies, utilities, magazine subscription people, and every one of the clerks has the answer to this question memorized. "Will you keep my social security number a secret if I give it to you?" They all answer, "Yes," because that's what they were told to answer. However, they don't work in the data base part of the company and maybe they really don't know.

The leakiest personal data-containing-buckets in the world are the credit agencies. They sell your personal information and get around the law by not including the credit information. The information they sell, however, contains your social security number, address, phone and sometimes, and often, a vital bit of info they can use to your distinct disadvantage, your mother's maiden name.

Opt out---which means restrict the credit agencies from giving out your information. In this case, you can call them. To make sure they get the message, read this over the phone to a responsible party. Ask for their email or mailing address and tell them you will send a copy of your opt(ion) out demand. I've never tried the single opt out call number. I recommend you call all three numbers and follow each call up in the mail, return receipt requested. Feel free to copy the forms from this chapter.

With a pen name on all your meaningless correspondence such as magazine subscriptions, utility and phone bills---with a P.O. Box receiving all meaningful mail and in use for driver's

Credit reporting agencies are the single biggest leak of your personal information. They circumvent the laws by supplying only header information---which includes your all-important social security number. Stop them from doing this by opting out.

ONE CALL---REMOVES ALL 800-353-0809

EQUIFAX 888-567-8688
Follow up letter: P.O. Box 740241, Atlanta, GA 30374

TRANS UNION 800-680-7293
Follow up letter: P.O. Box 949, Allen, TX 75013

EXPERIAN 800-353-0809
Follow up letter: P.O. Box 390, SPRINGFIELD, PA 19064

license, memberships, and all other organizations---with your social security number hidden from the world---with opt out from all credit agencies sent---with a shredder making confetti out of every personal document you toss---you have a chance that your identity will not be stolen.

TO: Equifax, Trans Union, and Experian,
This is to request that you remove my name, address, social security number, and any data you have on or about me from all lists you sell, market, or exchange with others as the law proscribes.
Please notify me by email, return mail, or phone message that this has been accomplished.
After sending this request, I will check to make sure you comply. Failure to comply would be cause for me to report the failure to the proper government authorities and to inquire with counsel if litigation could be initiated.
Sincerely,
NAME, FULL MAILING ADDRESS AND PHONE NUMBER

Check your credit rating every four months or so. Good protection looks ahead to the possibilities, and then creates defenses. I hope I've done that, but I can't see a long distance into the future.

If you discover unpaid bills, car payments behind on a $50,000 vehicle, some bounced checks, then you'll have the tedious job of rebuilding your good name.

Tell me what happened by writing email to pthfindr@gte.net. Dial www.survival-books.com and choose a free book; pay $4 postage and handling only.

In a few years, the bad guys will have discovered new ways to steal from us all. Possibly they'll hack into government lines and scoop out everything but your blood. It's conceivable that government would figure out a way to profit from the information it now gathers from super listening posts.

As it stands today, *somebody* knows all about you. Make changes on a regular basis and keep as many as you can guessing. Identity theft is like burglary. If your house is difficult to break into, they'll find an easier target. When they look for your personal data, I hope they discover who you (really) are:

Caspar, the friendly ghost.

FELONS. NO MORE ACCESS TO PUBLIC LANDS

If a judge can issue a restraining order to avoid a potential problem, why not restrict felons from lands other than what they own or lease? Moreover, if convicted on a felony charge, shouldn't the criminal lose access to public lands? The idea is to give citizens freedom to take a walk in a public park without fear.

How to enforce? ID checks by patrol with NCIC computer reports over the radio. Punishment for violation: Foreign prison. Convicts should have the freedom to roam all they want within prison parks, say, in Siberia.

Chapter 3

FORTIFYING YOUR CASTLE

When I first wrote this book, the major crime against your home was burglary. Since then, a number of HIR's have made a new crime a real reality. The letters stand for Home Invasion Robbery. Typically a gang enters your home, captures the whole family and then with knife to throat of a family member, forces the head of house to tell them where all the wealth is located. In addition to regular HIR's, we've now seen crimes where the gang follows a family member home and pulls into the driveway behind her. When she gets out of the car, they attack. Because most drivers attach house keys to car keys, they enter the house. Possibilities are: House robbery. Car theft. Rape.

> **NOISE TRAPS WARN YOU EARLY**
>
> When I worked as a San Diego cop, part of my job was to patrol park restrooms at night. My partner was street wise; he drove. We rolled up one night at 03:00 or so to a restroom around which a lot of fancy cars were parked. I opened my police car door silently and tippy-toed in, turned on my five cell flashlight. Full of men; but nothing going on illegal. I left. When I returned to the car, my partner interrogated me. "They knew you were on the way in because police shoes make noise on the sand which they throw on the concrete in front of the door."

I haven't seen any HIR defenses published. Nobody seems to have an answer. But you and I can develop one right now. How? Let's take the crime apart piece by piece. Then we'll figure out what we can do to eliminate it. Picture yourself as a victim. What went wrong? First, the germs had the element of surprise. Who would suspect an attack like this in one's own home? Second, they kidnap you. In essence, you are captured and held until you pay your own ransom. To summarize: They surprise you; they have more and better guns.

First then, let's deal with surprise. You need early warning. You have to expand the area around your home so it's like a de-militarized zone (between North and South Korea). Perhaps build a chain link fence or install a photo beam which rings a bell when broken. If you go for the fence, go for a dog or perhaps geese---either of which will warn you. At the fence gate, install a nine volt, battery operated intercom. Do not be visible from the street. Pull drapes at night. Light the outside of the home with sensor lights on all four sides. Allow no glass in the front door---which can be easily broken so that any intruder can reach through and unlock it. Use 3" deck screws on all security hardware. A front door brace such as shown in the illustration will keep intruders outside---at least long enough for you to retreat and arm yourself. Have one family member in charge of security. Begin with a check list until you know what all windows and doors are locked---with braces in place.

As soon as your area is violated by intruder, all house lights go off. Move all house members to sanctuary. Acquire basic weaponry such as a 12 gauge shotgun---with perhaps a load of #4 shot.

Now---should this develop into a "shots fired" situation, DO NOT EXPOSE YOURSELF. Several methods of delivering shot to a target remotely will keep you from becoming a target. Of course, call police, identify yourself and make sure the police know what you look like so no mistakes are made.

Still---the most common crime against your home is still plain old burglary, which takes less

Brace Detail

Door

Hardwood Pegs

Brace

Floor

DOOR BRACES FOR GROUND LEVEL ENTRY PROTECTION AT NIGHT

Note 4 x 4 oak or fir brace cut at 45° angles to fit against both door and floor. Once the brace is cut, drill, fit and glue hardwood dowels in the holes. Floor and door holes get no glue.

than five minutes and seldom endangers the home owner who is absent at the time of the crime. Forcible entry through a window is common, and most burglars actually penetrate the home from the front side.

Many pro burglars often plunder all night long, stealing from open cars and easy-to-enter homes with "burglarize-me" advertising on the front lawn such old newspapers accumulating. The average home in America is a pushover for any amateur burglar. Approximately 50% of burglars enter through an unlocked door or window. Others come in via an open garage. Your house may be locked, but if the garage is open, the burglar enters, shuts the garage door, and frequently uses the owner's tools to break in through a wall.

> ### INSPECT BY DAY---LIVE THERE AT NIGHT
> Real estate brokers normally show property during the day. Like it? Go back at night and take a look. Listen too. Loud Arguments? Drunken parties? Children beaten? Talk with potential neighbors. How many people occupy a nearby house? Sometimes it's ten foreigners who pay $100 a month each and sleep on the living room floor. Parking? What kinds of cars are there and how many? I don't recommend a real estate purchase in a neighborhood filled with primered cars parked on the street at night. Any bullet holes? Maybe you should live elsewhere.
>
> Do you have children? Visit school---20 minutes before it dismisses---so you can talk to neighborhood parents.

Typically, burglars rent storage lockers and then move the loot to another state before re-selling. One drug dealer in Florida sold crack for goods, then moved the goods to Georgia for a flea market sale.

Although many small American businesses fold after operating for less than a year, it often takes 5 years for police to catch a crafty burglar. One of those caught recently sneered at his sheriff captor as he went off to jail for a year, "I'll be back to get my stuff."

You can make your house absolutely impregnable, but you don't have to do that. Just make it a little harder to break into than your neighbors' houses and you've probably eliminated 90% of possible break-ins.

Contrary to other kinds of crime, a lot of burglary occurs during school hours. Watch the rate climb when teachers go on strike.

FORTIFICATION COSTS

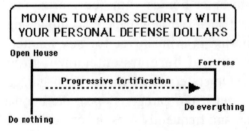

MOVING TOWARDS SECURITY WITH YOUR PERSONAL DEFENSE DOLLARS

Open House

Fortress

Progressive fortification

Do everything

Do nothing

Just as in the federal budget, make defense an on-going item in your budget. Thus, your house keeps getting safer. Newly developed security devices enable you to make your castle better fortified every month. Every bit of protection you add keeps you further away from violent conflict and invasion. Therefore, a defense budget is a priority item.

Like rape victims, many victims of **night intrusion.and home invasion robberies don't recover for years** Much of simple burglary happens during the day. If someone breaks into your house at night, they probably want more than possessions. Therefore, it's life-saving critical to block a night intrusion. General body guard instructions always dictate this: If you have to draw your firearm, spray gas or use a knife or baton, you made a mistake. Failing to prevent an intrusion to your home at night is the kind of mistake that leads to violence and lethal force. No matter who wins, you'll never get over it. Spend the money for the extra protection.

WHO'S THERE? PRO BURGLAR OR PSYCHOPATH?

Professional house burglars are not much of a personal threat; they try to avoid occupied homes. The real pros will often let themselves be caught rather than risk killing others or exposing themselves to becoming holey.

Therefore, if someone breaks into your house while you're at home, you can assume it is deadly serious trouble. Nobody can put a handle on what the psychos will do in your house. It could be rape or a murder just for the joy of it all. Others may break in to get money for drugs which makes them deadlier than a neuro-toxic snake. Most likely, whoever breaks into your home while you are there is prepared to kill you to get what they want. You have to consider this to be the worst case. This is the gravest extreme; be prepared mentally to handle it. Don't even think twice. If the guy is in your house while you're there, expect to send flying shotgun pellets in his direction.

William Goldman wrote this line in a movie called, *BUTCH CASSIDY AND THE SUNDANCE KID*. Sundance says, "One clear shot, just give me one clear shot. . ." I'm here to tell you right now---one clear shot is **stupid!** That's because to deliver one, you have to expose yourself to one. Don't do that! At worst, hold your shotgun around a corner and pull the trigger with your thumb after you duckbill the barrel. Better, set your shotgun in a solid core door hole and pull the trigger with a string from a safe location. Best: Electrical conduit can be bent to aim anywhere, and you can send pellets through it from a totally safe location.

In your home, you pretty much have the right to shoot. Shoot to **kill**—many times. A wounded perpetrator, aided by an attorney, will bring you years of trouble.

YOUR MOST VALUABLE ITEM

Some think jewelry; others, guns. But the one thing you need to protect is your home computer. That's because the hard drive normally contains all your personal financial data---which is far more valuable than anything a perp could carry if he happens to be connected to identity thieves.

Set up all your computers so they can't be booted up unless someone knows the password. That way, nobody gets your data.

Many computers have been stolen by common burglars for the value of the computer itself. Given the decrease in value of computer hardware, stealing the machine itself is a poor choice. Even so, it happens and your password protection may save you some real trouble because your data is worth far more than the computer.

Let me ask, "Is your data backed up and secure somewhere away from where you live? Just a zip drive stored in a friend's closet will save you a lot of trouble. If you keep personal and financial data on your hard drive without GOOD* password protection, your identity may be stolen. (GOOD* = name in foreign language only you would know) (BAD = your birthdate.)

Don't you wish you could simply buy a sign in a hardware store that would protect your home? We all see signs in local stores we think will help protect our homes. Oftentimes, however, the result is the opposite. I like a sign that says DO NOT DISTURB AT ANY TIME FOR ANY REASON. Call 742-9641 and leave a message. That's especially effective if your second phone is a voice mail service. Such a sign gives you an excuse for

36

never answering the door. You get no surprise visits and you don't have to listen to sales pitches. Still, friends and neighbors can contact you at will. Being a writer, I've already mortgaged my life. To maintain production, I need zero interruptions.

SIGNS FOR SECURITY

Any or all of these signs might help:

BEWARE OF DOG. Even if you don't own a canine a sign can be a real deterrent.

HOME PROTECTED BY SUPERIOR ALARM CO.

PROPERTY UNDER VIDEO SURVEILLANCE tells a burglar to smile; he's on candid camera. Any smile can and will be used against him in a court of law.

THIS HOME IS PROTECTED BY SHOTGUN THREE NIGHTS A WEEK, YOU GUESS WHICH THREE.

DO YOU BELIEVE IN LIFE AFTER DEATH? TRESPASS IN THIS HOUSE AND FIND OUT FOR SURE.

SIGNS OPPOSITE OF SECURITY

QUIET PLEASE. DAY SLEEPER announces someone is at home all day. Not such a good idea if you are single---because it means you work all night.

NRA MEMBER. Means you own guns! You've just become a prime attraction for every burglar who knows how to read letters of the alphabet.

CHAIN LINK FENCING

The U.S. government installs chain-link fence (6 ft.) and gates at driveways for security. Nothing is better. Set the posts deep into concrete. A single strand of electric fencing on top can be shocking.

Don't use solid wood or brick wall fencing. These give thieves and other outlaws the kind of privacy they crave. Five-foot-high, split rail fencing backed with 2x4 mesh "horse wire" makes a sturdy, attractive, hard-to-climb fence. A single strand of barbed wire wrapped loosely around the top rail of such a fence increases security effectiveness. Don't set anything outside your fence which would make the fence easy to climb.

EVEN WITHOUT FENCING

For your driveway, attractive stone or brick pillars allow you to hang lockable gates. This deprives thieves of vehicle access to your possessions. They don't

PILLARS FROM BRICK AND A LOCKING GATE

like to carry heavy TV's across the yard to a vehicle. Besides that, they don't want to be seen.

Invest in a safe deposit box at your local bank. Keep all your expensive jewelry, negotiable bonds, insurance papers, rare coins and other highly portable valuables in the bank's box.

Make an inventory of your possessions. Estimate what it would cost to replace them or insure them for full value.

BUILD A HOME SECURITY VAULT

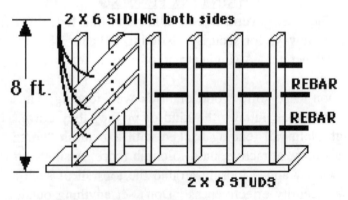

BUILDING YOUR OWN HOME VAULT

2 X 6 SIDING both sides

8 ft.

REBAR

REBAR

2 X 6 STUDS

Cover with plywood, both sides

The best locations are in a corner of your house—-on either the second floor or in the basement. A basement corner where the walls are back-filled on the outside is the most secure. It's also easier to build---only two new walls. Once built, it will be a strong, hard-to-violate security locker.

Use 2 x 6 studs. Drill the studs for electric wiring at knee height.   At waist height and perhaps other places, drill the studs and set rebar in through the holes. Cover both sides of the walls with diagonal 2 X 6. (If you use surplus lumber, treat for insects.) Next, solid sheet both sides with heavy duty plywood. Glue that plywood to the diagonal 2 X 6 with panel adhesive and nail it on with screw nails. Panel or paint the inside.

Hang a steel insert or solid core door only an archangel with Tomb-of-Jesus experience could penetrate.   The hinge pins go on the inside. This makes it nearly impossible for someone to force the door open or to tear it away from the frame. Put two (same key) dead bolts on it, one located a foot from the top of the door and the other located a foot and a half from the bottom. Install battery operated lights.

STEEL GUN SAFES are. .

a worthwhile investment for storing cameras, gold, jewelry and firearms. For double protection, put your gun safe into your home-built security vault.

DO NOT use the screws that come with the package of hinges and locks. I've personally tested these and found soft metal, poor design. Use deck screws. If you leave your original hinges on the door, that's fine, but change the screws! Cost; Pennies.   Just run the old screws out, run the new ones in. Labor cost: Minutes. Immense benefits. Deeper penetration, better holding power, stronger screw. Original screws are JUNK---so soft that the tool bit strips them. Also, too many threads with a shallow bite make them easy to pull.

USE solid core door

alwaysplace hinge pins on inside!

Five hinges are best. Remember, DECK SCREWS!

A SANCTUARY FOR FAMILY

In every; home, one room needs to be designated as a safe room, where any home resident can run and hide and lock the door securely. The best choice is a bedroom with a commanding view of the head of the stairs or the hall separating sleeping quarters from the rest of the home. Most often, that's your own master bedroom. Usually, it has a phone and a bathroom you can use as an inner sanctum with its own source of water and first aid gear.

Install solid core doors with dead bolt locks to make these areas secure. A cross bolt drop-in 2 X 4 makes the doors battering ram proof.

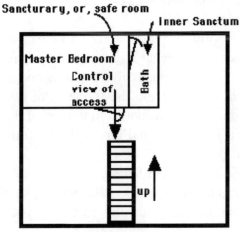

Sancturary, or, safe room

Inner Sanctum

Master Bedroom
Control
view of
access

Bath

up

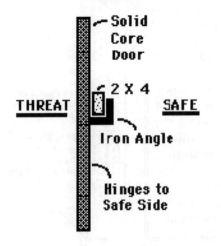

Solid
Core
Door

2 X 4

THREAT   SAFE

Iron Angle

Hinges to
Safe Side

Teach children to go to the sanctuary and lock the door when they think they're in danger. Pay special attention to window security in your sanctuary. On the ground floor, or if easily reached from any place on the roof, install stout grills on sanctuary windows. For windows two stories high with no outside access, include a chain or rope ladder so you can escape.

Take into account exceptional circumstances. Is there a handicapped member in your family? Maybe you'll use that person's room for a sanctuary or move the person to your master bedroom.

Home alarm systems prevent intrusions effectively. You arrive at home and punch in your secret number after entering. All is quiet. If you don't punch it in, an alarm goes off at a distant listening post. They call you. If you fail to answer coded questions accurately, they call police.

Our favorite home alarm system is called the Supervisor, from Transcience in Connecticut (**1-800-243-3494**). At #1, the alarm senses motion from an intruder which you turn off with a secret 4 digit number on your control keypad. If no code input, then #2, a monitoring system picks up trouble. It relays to a monitor station which calls the house to verify or calls police right away. Maybe police respond. We installed one of these systems ourselves and the thing works beautifully. As an added $150 option, you can have it sense smoke and call the fire department. We also added a panic button You save on installation by doing it yourself. After the company receives your floor plan, they tell you exactly where to locate and install everything.

www.transcience.com. on the internet.

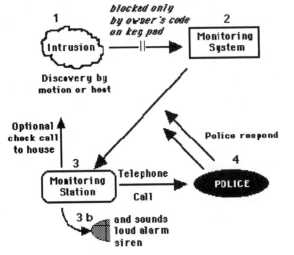

**TRANSCIENCE
Owner Installed
Alarm System**

1
Intrusion

blocked only
by owner's code
on key pad

2
Monitoring
System

Discovery by
motion or heat

Optional
check call
to house

Police respond

3
Monitoring
Station

Telephone
Call

4
POLICE

3 b

and sounds
loud alarm
siren

LIVE INTRUDERS?
Make this announcement:

"Listen carefully; there is nothing of value stored in this area of the house. There is a safe downstairs, and the combination is 36-12-25. Take what you want and leave. If you come towards this area, **we** will kill you." Never let on to someone who has broken into your home that you're alone. Examples: "We," not "I" and, "Our," not "My."

In addition to weapons, store two top quality flashlights with extra bulbs and batteries in your sanctuary. A portable cellular phone might be your most valuable aid. Call cops. Tell where you are located. Also, describe yourself over the phone so the cops don't mistake you for the burglar.

Don't expose a complete weapon to theft. Except defense firearms, store weapons in your vault room or gun safe. Store bolt action rifles with the bolts removed and semi-automatic pistols with the slides removed from the frames. Always store ammunition separately. Put the bolts and slides in a separate locking storage box. That way, a half weapon can't be fired.

THE INNER SANCTUM

Within your sanctuary, you need a special place where your children and others can wait out the event. With an extra layer of

---

LEARN FROM MY FAILURE

Situation. Son and I shared an apartment with fellow tennis pro student near Bollettieri's Tennis Academy in Bradenton Florida.

I failed to check the living arrangements of our neighbors in which six people lived in a two bedroom. One of those was hooked on crack cocaine.

He went up into his attic, crawled across to our attic access (no blocking wall) and dropped into our apartment, then robbed us blind to pay for his drug habit. Cops: No arrest. Too busy, proof poor. Warning from cops: "No fighting."

The best I could do was litigate in small claims court. In any case like this, don't sue the addict alone. Include all the residents of that unit (who knew or should have known that their roommate was a thief and did nothing to protect neighbors.) Include the property owner for accepting rent from stolen proceeds. With that kind of pressure, the thief was soon homeless.

---

protection between them and danger, they'll be out of harm's way. Once in, they need to stay there. If you get into trouble, they'll have to tough it out until help arrives. A bathroom will suffice. Just as with your sanctuary, pay special attention to the solid core door and window.

YOU'RE AT RISK HERE: IN YOUR OWN GARAGE

Garages are often hiding places for kids who take drugs. Worse, they hide attackers or burglars from street view. You would be in a bad tactical position of you opened your garage door with your car running and discovered a druggie or a home invasion group waiting to rob you. Electric openers are now necessary. Remember, stealing a garage door opener from your car in a parking lot is great gain for a thief who knows your address. How would he know that? Your auto registration. If they get the opener and your corresponding address, plan on company soon. They'll drive into your garage easily. Then with the door closed, many have used the home owner's tools to get into the house through the wall. After all, drywall is so easy to punch through.

SAFE GARAGE ENTRANCE PROCEDURES

Flood the garage with bright light by increasing the wattage in the opener's light bulb. Don't leave any place in the garage set up so someone could hide in there and wait for you. If part of the garage is blind to the driver, use mirrors and other lights. Open door; drive in. Turn off engine. Leave keys in ignition. From inside your (locked) parked car, activate your garage door to close. Look around your well- illuminated garage before you remove keys and exit your vehicle.

IN A RIOT?

At the first sign of trouble get out. Don't wait until the rioters are on your block to move. What a nice time to take a vacation. See if Motel Six left a light on. Do you have friends you can visit? Notify your family and police as soon as you're settled.

If you have time before you leave, secure all your valuables in your vault room. No vault room? Put your goodies in your bathrooms, push the lock button on the inside and close the door. Turn on a battery powered radio in that room to a talk station. Leave your TV on. Do the most you can to make looters think someone's home.

You may decide to stay and protect your home. Poor plan. It exposes you to danger in order to save a house you could rebuild and improve with insurance money. Do you have enough weapons, ammunition, emergency food and drinking water, a complete first aid kit, a small generator with fuel, plus several fire extinguishers? If you suspect incoming bullets may be flying, sandbags are a good idea. Most bullets will fly with ease through the average residence wall. If your house has a wood floor, don't forget a circular saw and a shovel or entrenching tool. Incoming bullets? Cut down through the floor and barricade the family within the concrete foundation walls. If the house goes up in flames, you can escape out through the crawl hole in the foundation wall.

TEENS! You will most likely take a set of keys to school, where you mix with other "students" from all kinds of backgrounds. Many take drugs.

Be VERY careful with your keys. At least ten percent of the kids in your school are taking drugs and wouldn't mind helping themselves to whatever your parents own.

One victim's keys were stolen in school, and his car was stolen during the night a while later.

The car was wrecked. Thieves were caught. No crime. Why? They told police that victim loaned them the car. Worse news. Since they had keys and claimed they borrowed, no insurance payment for the total loss.

***

The money you spend on various projects to keep you and your family safe from tragedy is the best investment you can make.

Your home is your castle, especially when you fortify it.

44

Y'all drive safe. . . Good advice, but hard to do what with road rage, robbers and carjackers.

We spend quite a bit of time in our vehicles. New crime waves have made that time dangerous. Carjacking became such a problem in New Orleans that the legislature made the killing of a carjacker justifiable homicide. Other crimes abound. Some criminals stage accidents on purpose to collect insurance by fraud. In Los Angeles, The Times reported that more than 90 hit 'n run accidents occur <u>daily.</u>

Don't attach your house keys to your car keys as most do. If you do, successful carjackers get a passport into your home. Why? Registrations with a home address tell them where you live. Hide your registration and keep your title in a safe place. If a police person wants to know who owns the car and whether the registration is current, a simple radio call gets him or her the answer.

Chapter 4

CRIMES AGAINST YOU 'N YOUR VEHICLE

We hear it often, "Drive safely." That used to send a message conveying good wishes in the hope that you wouldn't speed, wear your seat belt, and arrive alive. Now it means something else: Be wary of accident stagers who want to defraud insurance companies. Don't get carjacked. Watch out for road-rage.

More and more crime occurs to people while in and around vehicles. Rental car agencies now charge as much as $17 per day for insurance, a large part of which is for theft.

"But I always lock my rental car at night and park it in a well lit spot," I argued.

"Yes, but this insurance is for armed vehicle robbery," was the reply.

SITUATION REPORT

Just after the attack on two English tourists---one dead, one wounded---after someone tried to rob them. They were parked in the dark at a rest stop in Florida, when the perpetrator tapped on the windshield with a gun barrel.

Here's a question: How did the attacker know that this was a rental car and therefore contained tourists, probably foreign, who won't come back to testify even if the robber is apprehended?

It's because one of Florida's counties made a deal with the rental car agencies to sell plates cheaper than, say, Dade county which is really where the agency is located (Miami). Every crook in your State knows a tourist because the name of that county is printed on all license plates.

What's to learn from this? Don't take your car on a long trip to a tourist attraction if the license plate frames identify you as an out-of-towner. Car burglars will smack open the trunk because they know it's probably full of saleable items, like golf clubs. They also know you won't be back to testify against them if they get caught.

Carjacking is a crime in which the enemy gets your car, your purse, all the property you keep in your car, your house keys (if attached) and your address. Long ago, carjacking became a rite of passage for gang members. The germs steal your car, then

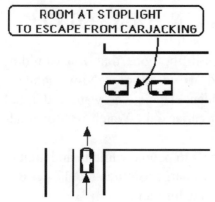

drive it around for a few days to show off. Of course, some do it for money. In a chop shop, parts off your car are worth more than double the value of the vehicle.

LOSING YOUR CAR WHILE DRIVING IT

Here's one way: You stop at a traffic light. Two germs team up. One steps off the curb in front of your car just as the light turns yellow. The other comes up from behind. With his back turned to traffic behind you, he taps on your window with a pistol and orders you out of the car. You get out quickly and run for your life. (Smart.) He jumps in and drives off. You think you should call for police to report your car stolen, but you must first think about your home security. Why? Your home address is probably printed on your auto registration in the glove compartment and he has your house keys. He may go there next. Call home and warn your family.

Take precautions against carjacking. For starters, detach your car keys from your house keys. Use a post office box mailing address on your auto registration. Of course, memorize your license number.

Improve your rear vision. Don't drive a car without a rear view mirror on the passenger side. It's a good idea to install a multi-window rear view mirror (Perhaps a WINK, from any auto store) so you can see all your blind spots.

If someone steps off the curb in front of you with obvious intent to block your forward passage, you can drive ahead slowly. The LAPD advises, "You're not driving your vehicle over someone if they have a chance to get out of the way." Once you see a move toward a weapon, step on the gas and go.

To prevent carjacking at a stoplight, leave some maneuvering space between you and the car ahead, say, half a car length. Practice that and develop the habit.

On occasion, some rapists imitate police cars with flashing red lights. Any doubts? Don't stop in a dark area; drive slowly ahead to a well lit, crowded area. No judge in the world would fault you for playing it safe.

WHEN MIGHT A BAD GUY ATTACK?

You're most vulnerable just as you get into, or out of, your car. That's when the germs like to hold you up at gun point, which can happen in a variety of circumstances. Most popular, the germs wait for the owners of ritzy cars parked far away from mall buildings. Rest stops and gas stations are also ambush places where the germs attack. Chances of being robbed go up in places such as poorly lit parking lots after hours and underground parking garages where you have to venture alone.

ESPECIALLY WOMEN . . .

Women are often mugging targets in underground parking garages. The perp wears sneakers and follows along silently out of sight. Long strides = tall woman (probably young and poor). Short steps = easier prey (probably older with money). The attack comes because perps know your back is turned while opening your door. You can fix that. 1. Tint your side windows and keep them clean so you can use them as mirrors. 2. Don't look at your door lock. Stand back at arms length and scan the reflections in your car door windows. Look for movement. Soften your focus; don't stare at one spot on your window, but look at the whole window all at once. Thus, you'll be able to see anything moving behind you. 3. Look around.

Remember too, take a quick look in the back seat before you climb into the car so you don't get in with a stowaway germ. If you make the mistake of driving away with an unwanted escort, crash the car---in traffic---preferably in front of a cop.

WOMEN
Tint the windows of the car you drive. The darker the better. If you're fair skinned, ask a dermatologist to write you a note so you can go darker than legal. Also, you can buy cheap pull down shades with a suction cup window attachment to give you privacy. Criminals are encouraged to attack when they see defenseless victims.
BLUE COLLAR HOLD UP
Take a knowledgeable man with you when you go for auto repairs. Many auto mechanics do work that isn't needed and charge you more than they could have gotten had they used a gun to rob you.

Some of the most heinous crimes occur when someone follows the victim home. Just as you get out of your car, they get you, your house keys, and free shopping in your house, before they drive away in your vehicle.

To prevent this from happening, adhere to the **rule of four turns.** From now on as you drive home, check out the visual profile of the car behind you. During the day you can observe the make, model, and occupants. During the night, you rely on street lights or your examination of the headlight-parking light configuration. Check to see if maybe one headlight is brighter in your rear view mirror because it's out of adjustment with the other. How wide set are the lights in the car? Drive slowly and silhouette the occupants when back lighting shows them up. Take notice of hats, hair, head heights, etc. Got it?

Now—- <u>make four right turns.</u> If the same car is behind you when you come back out on your original route, you have a problem. **Don't** drive home. Instead, drive to a police station, a highway patrol office, or the busiest gas station you know.

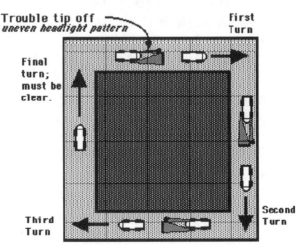

CARJACKING

How to give followers the slip
with the rule of four turns.

Trouble tip off —
uneven headlight pattern

First
Turn

Final
turn;
must be
clear.

Third
Turn

Second
Turn

RUSE: THEY HIT YOU FROM BEHIND

Perps often create a traffic accident by smacking you from behind. Knowing it's not your fault and being the good citizen you are, you pull over and step out to exchange insurance papers. According to the LAPD, the advice on what to do in that situation has been changed. Now you drive slowly and in orderly fashion to a crowded gas station before stepping out. Otherwise, you'll step out into a crime as the driver who bumped into you deliberately jumps into your vehicle and drives away.

One more caution: Don't let anybody come up to clean your windshield. If someone approaches with a spray bottle and towel, turn your windshield wipers on and warn him away.

CARJACK AND KIDNAP COMBINED

Listen to the words of the LAPD: "Don't give up your privacy." Don't get into any car at gun point; don't allow someone to get into the car with you. If a perp tries to force you into a car, just faint to the ground; go limp and become deadweight. If you take a bullet from a handgun in the city, your chances of survival are very good. Modern trauma centers have lots of gunshot experience and transport facilities are first class. Often the people who nurse you in an ambulance know as much as doctors did ten years ago. However, if you're left alone out in the country where help is not available, a simple stab wound with a short blade can cause death.

DON'T DRIVE IN TOUGH NEIGHBORHOODS

During one ten-day period in Oakland, California, 15 victims were beaten, shot at and robbed at the corner of 26th Street and Treat, a government project housing area. How? The oil can caper. The germs poured oil on the road so cars spun out; then they attacked and beat on the victims with baseball bats. They shot several others.

Also new and becoming popular is this: The germ goes into a restaurant or store and tells management, "Arizona License # DPJ-378, a tan, 92 Mercedes left the headlights on." Remedy: Think, "did I really leave my lights on?" Don't get up; it's an ambush. The germs are out in the parking lot---waiting for you. At gun point, they take your keys, then drive off in your Mercedes.

WHAT KINDS OF VEHICLES DO CARJACKERS LIKE?

When any kind of vehicle is popularly sold, it will be popularly stolen. For example, the Honda Accord. It also includes cars many people covet, but can't afford. So---high-ticket foreign sports cars offer the most tempting targets. If you buy one of these, perhaps ask the dealer if it also comes with a high-ticket handgun. Also, think of this: Where might your high ticket SUV be in severe demand? On mountain roads in undeveloped countries. Locally, thieves are stealing to satisfy demand. With altered papers, your car goes in a container to a buyer from South America.

WHO'S AT RISK?

Most criminals are male. How do they regard females? As weaker and easier victims. So female drivers attract more crime. Carjackers prefer single occupants. Baby on board? Some have threatened a child's life if you don't comply with their demands. Don't take these threats lightly. If they threaten you and don't follow through, they lose peer acceptance.

MAKE YOUR VEHICLE GOOD FOR SURVIVAL

Go to any public library and call up my Web--- www.survival-books.com and you'll see my book summary for *GREAT LIVIN IN GRUBBY TIMES* which contains the complete story on building a survival vehicle. One excellent primary vehicle is the SUV. I've always driven trucks, most of which were 4 X 4's. No matter what you choose, install an auxiliary gas tank to extend your cruising range to over 500 miles. Make a point of keeping the spare tank full. If you go the pickup route, consider a lift kit and big tires. Southland Corp. cut robberies in its 7-11 stores by raising the cash registers so robbers couldn't see the loot. In a perpetrator's mind, bigger vehicles with tinted windows make robbery a lot riskier. You might say, they don't try to rob someone they look up to.

VEHICLE EXTRAS

The average person doesn't make defense from crime a number one priority when choosing a vehicle, but it's a good idea.

Regardless of the kind of car you buy, it will be safer with certain options: Think security. Consider power windows and power door locks. Power steering and anti-lock brakes give you an advantage when maneuvering defensively.

This SUV or, Sports Utility Vehicle is extremely popular in the mountainous regions of many latin countries because of their four wheel drive ability. Therefore, it's a prime target for auto thieves.

If you buy a model which is a few years old, you save a lot of money. Add accessories. You can increase the survival aspects of this vehicle substantially (see *GREAT LIVIN' IN GRUBBY TIMES* .)

Now even Mercedes and Cadillac offer a sports utility vehicle. They roll more easily, but four wheel drive enables you to do some great tricks in survival. SUV owners don't practice off road enough.

Modifying this vehicle for survival doesn't take a whole lot. An extra battery in the rear, spotlights, communication equipment such as CB and cellular phone, a police band scanner, and kevlar inserts in the doors would be a good start. Don't forget to haul drinking water.

Get a sturdy, heavy-duty vehicle with plenty of carrying capacity and a large fuel tank. If it's a four wheeler, practice driving off road. You may have to evacuate your home during a civil disorder or natural disaster. Can you transport your whole family and the items you'll need for survival and comfort?

Along with all of the above, there are lots of things you can do to make your car safer and more theft proof. First, consider car burglary. Somebody wants your stereo, CB, etc. Defense: Leave nothing visible. Remember, <u>most vehicle theft occurs as</u>

opportunity presents itself. Keep your car's interior sterile of things to steal, even while underway. Mount your CB under the seat or in a compartment overhead.

How about car theft itself? The AUTOLOCK from Lawman Armor, is impressive. (Order 1-888-634-5750-about $60) Instead of adorning the steering wheel, this device locks the brake pedal or clutch with a barrel lock key (unpickable) so a new car won't go into gear. AUTOLOCK's steel is strong enough to withstand a hit from a shotgun slug. On the web: www.unbrakeable.com. Consider Lojack. Once installed, police can locate stolen cars easily. A satellite broadcasts the location.

Especially for women, keep your vehicle in first-class running condition because breaking down will expose you to

This actually happened to me in Point Loma, San Diego, Ca. June '75 in my big Ford 250 four wheeler, lifted. As a child of 38, I was paying too much attention to my well-dressed date when I accidentally cut off a car from Chula Vista in which four drunk gang members showed no sense of humor. They became enraged, especially after I insulted their ancestors.

They began chasing me. In the far left lane of a boulevard heading South, they pulled up right behind me at a red light. Two cars in front, I couldn't go forward. In truck's side mirrors, I saw all four doors open.

I made a left turn and easily rolled up over the concrete boulevard divider to go in the opposite direction. Low-riders can't go over curbs. They're probably still mad. So, "I wish to apologize for my poor driving, and stating that your parents were never married."

criminals, especially in populated areas. How many of the 84,000 convicted felons in California might drive by your broken down car in an hour? At a minimum, make sure your tires are in good shape, all the belts are sound and the fluid levels are up to par. Have your vehicle checked regularly and perform the recommended oil changes, lubrication, and regular tune ups. To me, the American Automobile Association is a great bargain.

SAFETY

Whether walking or driving, getting lost can create a situation in which you become a victim. Install a GuideTech compass (from WalMart and others) in your car to help you choose alternate routes. If you have a high riding SUV, I recommend the side bumper/steps. They protect you from severe injury in T-bone accidents, which are on the increase since more and more drivers try to beat the red light.

DRIVING STRATEGY

Men, quit driving. Let your wives drive; you ride shotgun. I equip my car car with a variety of pastime devices, including stereo radio, Bible, magazines, etc. to pass the time. If you possibly can, go everywhere in pairs. Women, especially, should drive with a LIFO companion. LIFO means Last In, First Out.

Carjacking from gas stations happens quite often. I guess it beats robbing the station for $200. If you drive into a station at night, drive around behind it before you stop at the pumps. Look for drunks and other misfits.

Drive into a parking lot or a gas station the same way a military patrol would come into an operational area. Scouts set up a perimeter. In this case, the man is the scout, and the perimeter is the visible area around the car. The man gets out of the car while the engine is still running and checks things out. If he comes under attack, he can either dive back into the car or return fire as the driver gets away. But the driver doesn't travel very far. She has options. She can call for help, raise hell with the car horn and lights, play bumper cars with perpetrators on foot, or get far enough away to fire with a long range weapon---like a rifle.

One way to maneuver you into a attackable position goes like this: The germs roll down their window and signal frantically to pull over because your tire is wobbling or you're leaking gas. When you pull over, they pull up behind to help---themselves---to your car and person. Don't pull over for anybody.

Another clever trick: The germs get a girlfriend with a baby to pull over to the side of the road and put the hood up. When you get out of your car to help, the perps come out of the bushes. Being a Good Samaritan is now a risky business.

POP QUIZ.

SITUATION: You come out of the mall to your new car parked far away to avoid door dents. As you approach, the car parked next to yours has two flat tires attended by a nicely dressed man who has his hands on his hips and is obviously frustrated. He makes eye contact and says, "Isn't this the worst? I have two flat tires and only one spare. I was wondering if you would be traveling in the direction of a gas station?"

Multiple choice: Answer Yes or No. (Circle one.)

If yes, you just bought yourself a lot of trouble. The guy poked holes in both tires himself. Not his car. Once he is in your car, he produces a pen knife and he owns you. Are you driving with a knife in your ribs? It's high time you had a good fender bender accident. You get extra credit if you crash in front of a cop!

Do not leave your auto registration in your glove compartment or over your visor. If you carry your registration in the vehicle, use a plastic baggie and hide it. For example, bury it under the rubber mats in the trunk, or tape it up under the dash. Why? Same reason you hide your garage door opener. Thieves in shopping malls search for garage door openers on your visor of your car by looking down at a mirror (on top of a book) as they walk past your car. Once discovered, they smash your car window to remove the opener and registration (with your home address). Almost immediately after that, they drive right into your garage to burglarize your house by using your tools to cut through the wall. Then they drive away and close the garage door behind them.

Don't attract attention to yourself or your car. Personalized license plates are a bad idea, especially for women. Lots of rapes occur because they give the rapist a feeling of conquest. Important women with personalized plates may appear to be a bigger conquest.

For the same reason discussions about religion and politics are to be avoided in social settings, avoid them in traffic. Be careful not to offend anyone on the road. But if you do make a mistake while driving, your chances of becoming involved in a violent confrontation remain less when you haven't posted additional insults on your bumper. Given the provocation of a bumper sticker condemning abortion, for example, you could experience some rude and aggressive driving, to say nothing of a fight.

LOCK YOUR DOORS

Your car is actually a fairly secure fortress if you make sure the doors are locked. Buckle your seat belt. It helps you stay in control if you have to do a bit of evasive driving. Make sure all your passengers are belted in, too, so they don't fly into you while your trying to get away. If someone does open your door and tries to pull you or anyone else from the vehicle, the seat belts will hold all of you in place while you step on the gas.

GAS STATION PRECAUTIONS

Try not to let your car's fuel level get too low. If you get into trouble with one of the growing number of morons on the interstate, you'll need extra gas.

Having a little extra fuel in the tank also allows you to keep driving if a chosen gas station features shady-looking characters. Make one trip to the cashier. Pay cash in

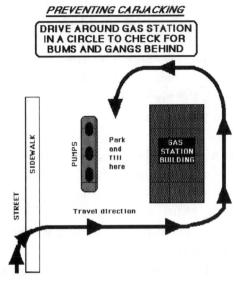

PREVENTING CARJACKING

DRIVE AROUND GAS STATION IN A CIRCLE TO CHECK FOR BUMS AND GANGS BEHIND

STREET

SIDEWALK

PUMPS

Park and fill here

GAS STATION BUILDING

Travel direction

advance and pump only that amount. Going back for change after you fill the tank exposes your car to theft for a longer time. Of course, do not leave your keys in the ignition; lock your car.

Where are you going? Tell somebody or leave a note. In our house we use cell phones, so we call home as soon as we're on the road and leave a message.

If your car breaks down, stay with the vehicle. Think of it as a turtle shell. If someone offers to give you a ride to a service station, decline. Hang a towel or scarf from your side mirror and wait for a state trooper or other emergency service vehicle. **Don't leave your vehicle.**

When you drive, pay close attention to what's happening on all four sides of your vehicle. Scan both side mirrors and your rear view. Don't follow other cars too closely. If you do, you'll pay too much attention to traffic ahead of you and break the good habit of scanning your rear view mirrors.

Many highway rest areas are now routinely patrolled by thieves and perverts. Homeless people often live there. Avoid public restrooms. If you absolutely need a rest room, restaurants and truck stops are safer than public facilities. Men: Avoid urinals. You're extremely vulnerable to attack when standing with your back to the world in that circumstance. Use the toilet compartments and lock the door behind you. If no door, stand to the side. Thieves look first for a pair of pants dropped around shoes. Then they quietly climb on the seat in the next stall to check the hook. This is not the best way to be robbed. Women who put purses on the floor or hang them on a hook run the same risk. Other females (perhaps homeless) prey upon rest stop travelers. It's best to carry a purse with a shoulder strap and hang it around your neck. Don't set your purse on the sink either. Keep it securely on your person.

Above all, **DON`T PICK UP HITCHHIKERS!** Thousands of bright people make this mistake each year; some pay with their lives. In many states it's not only against the law to hitchhike, it's against the law to pick them up. Don't be fooled by the gas can trick, either. Real criminals know how to make themselves look most pathetic.

The risks on the highway are just too great for good Samaritans. Don't stop on the highway to give assistance to a stranded motorist. Even someone lying on the road could be setting a trap for you. Use a phone or a CB radio if you see someone in trouble.

***

All of us have long thought of our cars as private places. That's no longer true. Drivers are easy prey for criminals. But if you turn up your perception knob, make a few additions to your vehicle, and stay locked behind tinted glass, you can avoid almost all highway robbers and street thugs.

Chapter 5

NON-SHOOTING WEAPONS

Rule #1: Avoid contact, and therefore combat with a criminal. Rule #2: Win <u>decisively</u> any fights you can't avoid. To do that, you need to have weapons superiority. If you're a belted Karate player, you'll probably win (although suffer some damage) as long as the conflict remains hand-to-hand. However, most criminals cheat and once they employ any weaponry, any Karate artist could easily lose.

Weapons don't make you invincible. They only help. In *EVERYBODY'S OUTDOOR SURVIVAL GUIDE*, Green Beret silver star winner Rick Woodcroft gives us the definition of a weapon: "Any thing that lengthens or strengthens your sphere of defense."

I discuss firearms in the last chapter of this book. Properly employed, they represent the best defense. While appearing on over 250 media shows on this subject, I'll bet two dozen people asked me questions about guns. One little woman under 100 pounds wanted a .44 magnum. An apartment resident told how he created a new pass-through window to his neighbors bedroom with a shotgun. Like these, most think guns can save them. That's true, but you have to practice. If you buy one and leave it in a drawer or closet, you could shoot and miss, or perhaps shoot and kill---the wrong person, which is why LAPD has multiple civil suits pending. Once the bullet flies, it's out of your control.

Of course, you have to learn how to use any weapon you employ. If you arm yourself with a ten-pound baseball bat, (beyond your muscle ability), you'll be extremely slow and some quick judo guy will step in close and throw you. Pepper spray is wonderful---unless you spray it into an oncoming wind. Also, consider the other side's capability. Don't face up to a firearm with a stick. Situations like that come about when you pull the stick and the other side surprises you with a cannon. When faced with a handgun, you'll need a rifle or shotgun to maintain an advantage; otherwise you'll finish second in a field of two.

Finally, consider the damage you might suffer. Winning makes little sense if it causes you permanent injury. Understand also, that if you use a firearm in the face of a threat not considered lethal, you could face prosecution.

WHY A NON-SHOOTING WEAPON?

After the second edition of this book, I met numerous people who hated guns. There is simply no way they would learn to handle, much less buy, a firearm. Even for many of us who do practice shooting, carrying is only legally feasible in 31 states. Thus you might not have a handgun with you when the need arises. So knowing how to defend yourself with something other than a firearm is a good idea.

Let's consider your non-shooting options. To do that, first understand the elements of combat. Before you choose a weapon, consider **range, speed, power, control, target accuracy, and**

operational convenience. Apply these elements to your own strength and ability.

Range. This term defines the distance to a given target. If you keep an opponent at a distance where he can't hit you but you can hit him, you win. Examples: Your legs are longer than his arms so you can kick; your sword or spear is longer than his knife; your Bo (five-foot hardwood shaft) will reach out better than his short club. In all of the above examples, however, the range could change quickly. Then you have problems. In close, the stick beats the bo, the knife beats the sword. Long legs have to bend to become short range weapons called knees. Elbows do the same. Generally however, the longer the range, the safer you'll be. You risk personal injury any time an assailant gets close to you.

Speed. Quickness counts a lot. If you can move faster than your opponent, you'll score and do some damage before he does. So, a weapon enabling you to strike fast is a good idea. For example, you can pool-cue quickly with your Bo so the blow lands before a block can deflect it. Note also, you have to be fast enough to get your Bo back out of there before he can grab. Don't choose a weapon you can't control. Lose your weapon in a fight and your assailant gains the advantage you thought you had.

Power. You have to deliver sufficient force with a blow to make your influence felt. A severe bruise or opened blood vessel generally means you've done damage (as opposed to only pain). On the other hand, minor bruise or pain merely gets your opponent's adrenaline flowing. Read Rick Woodcroft's chapter on hand-to-hand combat in *EVERYBODY'S OUTDOOR SURVIVAL GUIDE* and you will learn that the best blows are delivered to the weakest areas on your opponent's body---with force.

Target accuracy. All humans have delicate target areas. Smacking hard on his shoulder won't help you much. The same force to the throat or groin is more persuasive. Some weapons are easier to direct accurately on a desired body target than others. You can produce pain, deliver damage or cause death. Of course, your choice may have legal consequences.

61

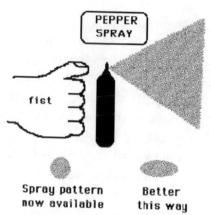

PEPPER SPRAY

fist

Spray pattern
now available

Better
this way

You can buy an inert trainer in many places. Check the pattern just as you would with a shotgun.

Spray pattern on right makes much more sense. The idea, spray into perp's face at a distance.

Operational convenience. Does it take two hands or one to make your weapon work for you? Can you make it readily available or do you have to unpack and unfold it? How much muscle do you need to cause this weapon to work righteously? If only one hand is required, can you use a separate weapon in the other? Consider your personal ability. Whether you're tall and strong or short and weak, some kinds of weapons will work better for you.

<u>DEFENSIVE SPRAY GAS</u>

The best way to counter an attack if you don't want to shoot somebody is to spray gas. You don't need to be strong, you can hit from a distance and you need only one hand. I favor the cheap pepper formula, which temporarily blinds your assailant. Don't leave home without spray gas, unless you fly by commercial air where depressurization can cause a gas leak in your suitcase.

Spray is one of the better **women's** defense tools. Take the spray canister out of your purse and hold it in your hand anytime you have to go into dangerous territory. Examples: Underground and shopping mall parking areas, hospital parking lots, and any place where a variety of low-lifes gather.

Modify the can with glue-on plastic or a velcro stickie so you can feel it in the dark. That way, you won't spray backwards into your own face.

Learn to spray with your non-dominant hand. That frees your (right?) hand to open doors, carry car keys, or perhaps access a more powerful weapon---like a handgun. Any perpetrator you spray who continues to attack gives you reason to be scared for your life, which makes violent force legally acceptable almost everywhere. Shoot. For those assailants too drugged up to succumb to gas, let lead persuade.

MAKIWARA STICK

fist

total hammer fist power transmitted at this point

KEY CHAINS KEYED TO DEFENSE

Women: Set up your car keys like this: Purchase a large, strong key ring. A short hardwood stick about six inches long brings the full force of your hammer fist to a sharp point. Attach a two ounce fishing sinker to your key ring so you can use the stick as a handle, and the sinker as moral influence.

If you don't modify your key chain, purchase a rubber cover for the head of your longest key. Then learn to carry your keys with the point (sharpened is OK; the key will still work in locks) protruding between your fingers when your fist is closed. You can protect your palm further by backing up the protruding key with a handkerchief.

LONG RANGE HELP

The Bo. My favorite. Usually, you make yours as long as you are, but not wider than the inside of your car so you can store it behind the

MEASURING THE STAFF OF LIFE FOR A STREET FIGHTER

Proper length for the Bo

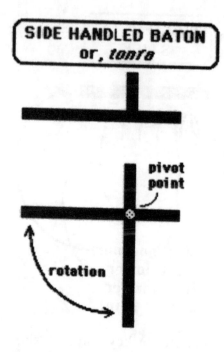

SIDE HANDLED BATON
or, *tonfa*

pivot point

rotation

seat. How? Buy a round oak dowel and trim down the ends. You can also make these from a hardwood tree limb. Viney maple makes an excellent choice, as does oak. Cut the maple or oak limb so you have a sort of shepherd's crook on one end to use on your attacker's ankles and knees. Using a Bo requires two hands. After only a few lessons from a martial artist, a bo will put you in command of almost all combat. Carry your bo while jogging through any residential neighborhood; you'll soon appreciate how you can use it as a teaching aid. It will teach terrific tricks to the dumbest dogs, like---roll over and play dead.

A major TV station paid my way to San Francisco to appear on their morning show. I took a Bo along. The host for the show got a little macho with me and said, "What if I block it aside like this." I retracted the Bo so he missed the block, then pool-cue jabbed him in the chest with it. Sorry; too much muscle. He was bruised for awhile.

COPS' CHOICE

The Tonfa. This is the PR-24 or side-handled baton. You can make one or buy one made out of aluminum. Requires only one hand. You need lots of practice because this weapon can come back on you and do some damage. Police trainees routinely break their upper arms with one of these. Once you learn to use it, however, you turn into a tank. But you need to close the range to make it perform, which could cause you to suffer some damage. Best swing to practice here is to fake high and swing low across the knees from the side.

CUTTING TOOLS

Path Finder still sells my *EVERYBODY'S KNIFE BIBLE* in which I teach you how to use knives as tools rather than fighting weapons. Women especially should be advised: Most criminals have knife-fighting experience and believe that a woman with a knife challenges their macho image. Threaten a germ with a knife and he'll be compelled to take the conflict to the limit to avoid humiliation.

Also, don't bring a knife to a gunfight. Once you pull a knife, you escalate the disagreement to the level of lethal. If the other side of the argument has a gun, learn to pray quickly.

Machetes. Long blades make them like swords. They're a little slow. Some of the cheaper ones are high carbon steel and rust easily along the cutting edge so the blade becomes dull. See *EVERYBODY'S KNIFE BIBLE.*

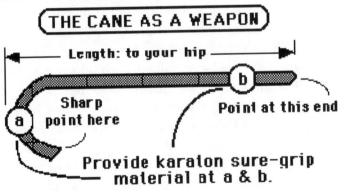

THE CANE AS A WEAPON

Length: to your hip

Sharp point here

b

Point at this end

Provide karaton sure-grip material at a & b.

FOR OLD FOLKS. READY ALWAYS

Use a cane if you have trouble walking. If you turn it around, you can hook any ankle and pull an assailant off balance. Pool-cue the straight end into somebody's abdomen and the fight is generally yours. An umbrella does the same. The more pointed the end is, the deeper into the body it will penetrate.

DEALING WITH CRIME---
THE EN-LIGHTENING METHOD

Buy a solid, metal, five- (maybe four-) cell police-type (We like the Mag Lite) flashlight. Either C or D batteries give this

> Put sharp points at both ends because this is a jabbing tool or [when held at (b)] an excellent tool for hooking the ankle of your opponent and pulling it upwards toward you. Such a move keeps you at safe range and disables your opponent. Sharp point at curved end allows you to hook clothing or anything else you care to penetrate.
>
> Learn to foot-sweep. You bring your kicking foot from the side and take out a leg. If you first lift one leg high with your cane and sweep the other, your opponent will experience the frustration of being a one-legged man in a kicking contest.

the weight you need to persuade an attacker to give up his vocation. Place this flashlight under the seat of your car; it's a great deterrent---just the sight of these things scare a lot of career criminals because of memorable police encounters. If you really want a criminal to see the light, hit him with a five-cell steel flashlight.

Use metal tube flashlights the same as you would use with a stick. Turned sideways and held with two hands, you can block all kinds of incoming blows. Raised over your head to strike, however, you'll be exposed and open to damage. The best strike with this light is the pool-cue plunge, but it also works well like a baseball bat at the knees. The beauty of using this tool to come across the knees from the side is the tremendous whip you get because the flare on the bulb end keeps your hand from slipping. Without that, you could only hold on with your grip, so the speed of the blow would not be as fast. Only one hand operates this in striking mode, use something in your other hand; for example spray gas.

CRIME CAN BE SHOCKING

You deliver 200,000 volts out of some of the electrical shockers to bring many criminals to a sagging heap on the floor. I'm not impressed with lower voltages. I watched a Navy Seal at the SHOT Show one year get zapped in the elbow and he turned around and said, "Can I help you?" If you remember Stacey Koon, the police officer who went to jail after the Rodney King incident (Los Angeles criminal who won three million is subsequent lawsuit) he said, "We tazed him twice with no effect."

Besides the jolt sometimes having very little effect on a criminal, you have to get in close to apply the current. That could be dangerous.

GETTING TO THE NITTY GRITTY

Sand or dirt. Flick sand or dirt into your opponent's face. The idea is to land it in the eyes, but you gain an advantage even if it only causes him to blink. Follow the sand flick with some decent kicks and blows---perhaps with your flashlight.

ROCK-A-BYE BABY

How's your arm? Can you throw with speed and accuracy? Don't forget stones. It only takes a few of these to provide ammunition you can use effectively before your target ever gets close. Ammunition costs nothing, and practice is fun. You can also roll a rock into a towel to create a good weapon. A (smooth) rock in your sock also does well. Rough rocks, like chunks of broken concrete can be wrapped in a web belt. Be careful, however. Swinging anything heavy on a rope, stick or towel can cause it to come back and hit you.

WEAPONS GENERAL EFFECTIVENESS

Any of these weapons can give you an edge if you have to go to combat. Also, a confident stance with one of these weapons will often be enough to scare an attacker away. Most criminals don't fear jail; they fear bodily harm. When you have a weapon and a willingness to use it, your posture will be more erect, your stare steady and offensive, and your balanced body weight will indicate confidence. Any street fighter recognizes these signs as trouble. Therefore flashing any one of these weapons may be enough to avoid a struggle. However, don't fake it with a weapon you are unwilling or don't know how to use. Criminals read that too.

One last item: All weapons, whether they be non-shooting or firearms, have a position in a hierarchy. You can't go against any superior weapon with a decent hope of surviving. Baseball bats always do better than a rock in a sock. A Bo is faster than, and can out-range a baseball bat. Knives are wonderful, but you have to attach them to something to give you range. Then they're called spears.

Bare hands come in last. That's because weapons are extensions of your own ability to fight, and almost always enhance it upwards by several grades. Only in the movies will you see a karate guy disarm someone with a knife. If you try it, suture self.

Specialize. Find one weapon that matches your quickness, strength, and the range you need. Then practice more and often. Realize, however, that you and this weapon have limitations.

When you add the price of medical rehabilitation for injury to the price of goods stolen after you get hurt, you'll understand right away---you're better off to let them have what they want instead of risking your corpus to protect it. But if you have to protect a loved one, do it with the enthusiasm and the effectiveness a weapon can provide.

In the movie, *PATTON,* he begins by telling his troops, "You don't win wars by dying for your country. You win a war by making some other poor bastard die for his country."

Let me adopt that for the streets. Never get into a squabble where you have a chance of suffering severe physical damage.

Conquering crime isn't about dying for your community; it's about making a criminal die or at least go to prison for his.

CHAPTER 6

CRIMES AGAINST SINGLES

During the late 80's, I moved to Florida where I interviewed a large number of widows. If you combined all of these women into one, her story goes like this: During the 30's, she was a beautiful young women approximately 20 years old who was approached by a number of men---all of whom brought flowers or candy. They proposed. Many were on their knees. The pitch went: "_____, I love you with all my heart and I want to be your husband for the rest of my life. I'll work hard, bring home my paycheck, help raise the children, be faithful and true. All that I am and ever will be is yours for life."

She chose one of her many suitors. She married and lived happily ever after until he died and left her to be a widow---which is when I interviewed her. During her life she experienced some events and emotions which most modern women will never know.

A. Constant devotion and care from a <u>faithful</u> husband who's actions throughout his life proved she was his life-long queen and the precious love of his life.

B. Family reunions in which great and grand children came to her with the most intense love imaginable.

C. Cheating in marriage was unheard of. So both husband and wife lived in a loving and secure physical relationship with each other, because both had saved themselves to present a virgin to the one they chose to love for life.

Today, modern Marilyn has a different experience. Over half suffer through a divorce, poverty, and a painful aftermath. She socializes primarily with "singles." She reads single magazines, goes to singles dances, dates divorced men, and plays the singles game.

WOMEN ALONE

Single women are a target for robbery, rape, theft, carjack, cons, assault, battery, purse snatch and murder. They're perceived to be weaker, and easier to scare. Besides, the perp worries less about getting hurt. Also, many perps turn to crime because they had dysfunctional relationships with the only parent around--- mother. Psychologists tell us of one prevalent reason: Aggression transfer. The 30 something husband leaves the nest for a 20 year-old lollipop. The 10 year old boy he leaves with mom looks and talks just like his father---at whom mom is really miffed. So the boy catches all the flak the mother really wants to heap on the father. When the boy grows up, any woman is a potential scapegoat. The added vengeful power trip of rape is also a potential threat.

Purse snatching isn't particularly profitable, but it's popular because it's easy and simple. You don't need a brain to grab a purse and run. Think about the psychological state of the perpetrator. Many street robbers are just coming down off their latest drug binge. To say the least, it makes them moody. They don't have time to figure out a complicated crime. They need— now, and women's purses are everywhere, so they grab and go.

Subway perps often stand near their victim and grab the purse just before the doors close. The perp walks free as if nothing happened. On the street, it happens all the time; that's why women need to walk against traffic as well as the directional arrows painted on parking lots. Some germ hero can't hang out a car window and grab from behind you.

Don't dangle bait (your purse) in front of a drug addict. Hide your purse! Attach a long carrying strap to your purse. It goes over your shoulder, under your coat.

Don't carry your house keys and ID in you purse. If they get your purse with ID and keys, they'll pick you clean at your home address without having to break in. If you're carrying something valuable, and it looks as if you're being stalked, you can ditch your purse in any mail box and get it back from the post office later. Also, forget carrying an expensive bag. Buy a nylon belt purse (also called a fanny pack) and buckle it around your waist. If you don't feel comfortable without a purse, spread most of your money and credit cards around. Inside shirt and coat pockets make good stash places. So do the tops of socks.

Don't get out of your car without scanning your mirrors and taking a good look around. Boy friends: Be this woman's LIFO, (Last In, First Out). She gets into the car first to drive while you scan the perimeter. When you arrive, check first for potential dangers before you get out of the car to make her safe exit secure. Trouble? She gets back in the car and drives away. You stay and decoy the problem.

Thus, no matter where you are, you'll have to become more security conscious. Lock your doors everywhere. Don't make unnecessary trips anywhere. Don't go into major cities without a companion. Stay behind curtains at home. Hide behind tinted windows in your car. Finally, watch your telephone security. Give out no information; talk to no strangers; and don't allow strangers into your space.

If your car breaks down, **do not** accept help from strangers. The slightest social contact with some men who stop to help a lady can be trouble. Once your car is fixed, they think you owe them.

DATING CAN BE DANGEROUS

> If ads in singles newspapers required absolute truth, most men would have to word the ad like this: *Do you like thrift shops and garage sales? If so, marry me; I am 50% off.*

Go with me on this analogy. As young girls mature, they drag their magnets though a sandbox. The sand granules are the young men with whom they come in contact. Pull the magnets out of the sand, and a certain portion of the iron ferrites in the box are attached---lured, if you will, by each young girl's magnet. At age 20, the sandbox is filled with possibles---men of high character, self control, caring, committed, dedicated with the ability to love from the heart. Once divorced, however, the women, perhaps with children, go back to the sandbox again where they encounter cast-offs, men who likewise lost in the game of marital relationships. Collectively, their character is low. Many drink, have lost control of self, and have fallen prey to a number of evils the world has to offer. Many are bitter about their divorce losses and transfer their aggressions onto each new female conquest.

> Perhaps my own experience tells it like it is. I was a volunteer worker for 800-HIT-HOME, a call-in-ministry for children under 18 who were in trouble. One raped and beaten teen girl called from Florida. Her abuser was mother's boyfriend and a cop.
> My pastor talks to the mother who refused to believe her daughter was raped. Finally, she broke down and told him in tears, "Do you know how hard it is to find a boyfriend?"

While the woman believes this new man is attracted only to her, the reality is: Rejection and insecurity make men horny. "Any port in a storm," is what really makes her feel so special and desired. The atmosphere all around this new couple with "chemistry" is charged with sex, and more sex. Music, advertising, TV shows and ads, magazines, movies and humor are built around sexual longing.

Some men have become sexual predators. In a world in which many women have "given sex to try and get love," the men have "feigned love in order to get sex." As the comedian George Gobel once quipped, "East is East and West is West, and never the twain shall meet---unless they get on the same twack." In the

> I went to a PWP meeting (Parents Without Partners) on Oahu, Hawaii. I spoke to the man sitting next to me. He was a psychiatrist---still married and just playing around. He said, "There's a lot of great looking and needy women here." I can guess---that later on, he told some great looking woman, "Trust me; I'm a doctor."

world of singles, that twack doesn't happen very often. Men have allowed sexual appetites to grow beyond limit as they sample the sea of available women for a night or two. "I don't want to get involved," is something a single woman hears repetitively. The choices are: A. Try not to get emotionally involved and play the field so your feelings are never hurt. B. Risk love. The search for love intensifies. It's competitive, which is why singles spend billions for cosmetic surgery.

ARE YOU SAFE IF SINGLE?

> Some suitors and ex-spouses can become persistent, even violent. One remedy is for the single girl to go to court and
> GET A TEMPORARY RESTRAINING ORDER (TRO)?
> Yes if, the persistent guy is a suitor. The court order will work because his emotional investment isn't deep and whatever he got from you can be replaced.
> No, if this is a husband with whom the emotional investment is heavy, you have children together, plus years behind you. A TRO spells END for many, and your ex may kill you. It happens often.

Fact: In the late 80's, the Surgeon General of the United States cited violence as the leading cause of injury to women between 15 and 44. That means you are more at risk of harm from personal violence than you are from muggings, auto accidents and cancer.

Now---given that so many bad people are in the divorced category, what do they act and look like? Wonderful. "Mahvelous." They're often witty, intelligent and gorgeous. Divorced people can outdo the Devil when it comes to deception. Cosmetic surgery, make-up, hair coloring, facial treatments, skin tighteners, gyms and tanning booths make all manage to look their best. Various schools all across the country teach men and women the art of flirtation. One particular school in Hollywood teaches seduction for $800.

After packaging themselves like the professional singles they are, would they relate anything bad in their history? Not quite. Like a prison full of criminals, all of them here at this singles' dance are totally faultless in their divorce and their attorneys screwed them. They present themselves as victims, and as the wail of several songs go, "they NEED your love" because "you're so special." In reality, they need to copulate worse than a goat on viagra. You'll do. Especially after a few drinks.

How do children fare in this atmosphere? Florida, for example, reported that child abuse is the cause of one out of five children's deaths. Step parents and partners frequently see the child as an obstruction to happiness. Teen girls often suffer sexual abuse. Run-away teens number in the thousands, and the major cause is parents or live-in lovers who are abusive.

Are you thinking about relationship? As if this person were about to become your employee, you've got to do your investigative homework. Look for outright lies and character faults. If your "friend" has lived for a long time in one county, then State and County records may provide enough information. If he or she moves around a lot and has no steady record of employment, Federal records are available. Following is a list of public and government agencies you can check.

You begin by learning your friend's social security number. To make an I.D. positive, it's also helpful to obtain a date of birth. That date also appears on a driver's license, but is not mandatory. Many women legally refuse to publish their age.

If you can't obtain a Social Security number, this person may be trouble. Does he rent or own the property in which he lives? If he says he owns, county records will confirm that. It also will reveal any other address he may have---where the tax bill is sent and where his wife and children may live!

ASK DMV?

A phony driver's license is the most commonly used documentation for those who steal others' identities. You can

---

NICOLE SIMPSON was not allowed by the laws of Los Angeles to protect herself. She couldn't get a gun permit. She couldn't (at the time) buy pepper gas unless she took a course.

contact the Motor Vehicle Departments of any state he says he lived in and obtain his driving records. You can also learn what vehicles he or she really owns. Drunk driving or reckless driving citations will show. Vehicles may be registered at an address different than your friend's residence---like his family address.

If your "friend" has an occupation for which a license is required, check with the licensing agency. From Aircraft mechanic to X-ray technician, the controlling agency will supply you with the name of any spouse, the time he obtained his first license, and his addresses.

Did he go to college? You're entitled to find out his permanent and local address, and whether or not he played on any athletic teams. If he owned a boat or hunted or fished with a license, information is available.

Was your guy in the military? You can get a list of the active duty military schools he attended and his past duty assignments. What about prison or jail records? If your man went to jail or prison, records are available.

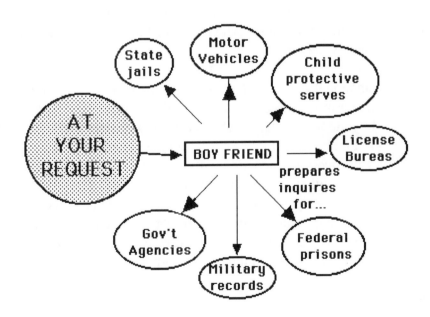

While these are not all of the ways to check, they provide you with a base. Most important, probably, to any single mother, is knowing whether her guy has had previous problems with a child abuse or non-payment agency. If he had a problem of abuse with a minor, the minor was picked up by the state's child protective services and the offender was listed.

Does he balk? Just the thought of you checking should be enough to send him on his way. Either way, you'll sleep a lot more soundly when you know that your beau---is on the level.

WOULD YOU MARRY A HOT FOREIGNER?

After divorcing an American, you might think a foreign-born new spouse might be a better second choice. Cherry Blossoms and other foreign dating services are booming.

Divorces cause hurt feelings. Depriving a parent from children is the ultimate vindictive punishment one can inflict. Be careful! During a second divorce, the foreign spouse frequently opts to kidnap the offspring and head back to the country of origin, in which event, recapturing the child by the American parent is next to impossible.

At this writing, over 10,000 American born children are residing abroad with spouses who kidnapped them. The American parent is nearly helpless. . .

***

Emotional pain is not the only problem with being alone. You're also a more attractive target. Half the time your home is empty. In your car, you have nobody to help with defense.

If a remarriage doesn't appear on your horizon, I suggest a dog. It will love you unconditionally as if its name were spelled backwards. It will also take a bite out of crime.

As soon as you're on your own, turn up your perception knobs. Make sure your defenses are in place. One big advantage of being alone is freedom to choose. Take extra precautions with all the choices you have and thus choose---never to be a victim.

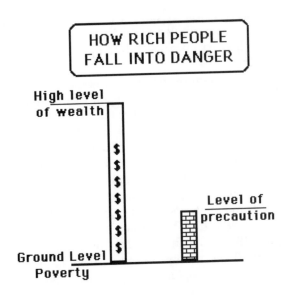

CHAPTER 7

WHEN YOU ACQUIRE WEALTH . . .

Generally, successful businessmen and women are too busy to notice the growing danger from the wealth they've accumulated. They live in complacency they knew from the early days, when they were relatively poor. Because they, themselves, work hard and earn the rewards, they don't understand others who envy them and covet what they have. Thus, the increasing risk of victimization and the danger it brings creeps up on them.

If you've made money, face the fact: Everybody wants what you have. I've followed several cases in which wealthy people were targeted---by criminals, by lawsuits, by employees, by spouses, and sometimes by reputable business firms. **When "people" find out you have money, they come after it.** The maxim for keeping what you acquire without personal risk is this: **You must take precautions in direct proportion to the wealth you accumulate.**

Disgruntled male divorcee: "I now have to pay-to-play with my children---because I didn't pay-to-play enough with my childrens' mother.

Pre-nups, or, pre-nuptial agreements are common. It would appear to the poorer of the pair that the pending marriage begins in a spirit of distrust. If you're the richer of the two, however, present the idea this way: "I want us to be together forever. Being human, we may have some bad days. To get past those bad days, we don't want an attorney to look at the profit in a divorce action."

Many marriages have ended because one spouse was told, "I can make you rich." So, she files, the attorneys get a real war going, costs mount, trials are long, and the battle over assets helps to create a WAR OF THE ROSES, (movie). After the divorce, her newly acquired wealth slipped through her fingers (a fool and her money are soon parted) and she lives alone in poverty. Often, both wish the divorce had never happened and it never would have, but for the fact that assets were involved. "Good pre-nups help solve this problem," attorney Mike Green, Chula Vista, Ca.

REAL CRIMES

As you acquire more wealth, these are some of the crimes of increasing appeal to those around you.

<u>Burglary</u>. Better house in a wealthier area. Therefore, more saleable goods in the home. Safe cracking during burglary. Art, antique and jewel thieves will consider you as a prospect.

<u>Employee theft.</u> They figure you have it and won't miss it.

<u>Get rich quick schemes.</u> The lure of fast money appeals to rich folks who have tasted success and are eager for more.

<u>Extortion</u> You are threatened personally if you don't pay.

<u>Armed robbery</u> Your money or your life seems like an appropriate pitch by someone who figures money doesn't mean much to a wealthy person.

<u>Identity theft</u> **Opt out!** (See chapter in this book). Develop an alias. Use low limit cards for phone orders. Guard your Social Security Number better than they guard Ft. Knox.

<u>Kidnapping.</u> Rich folks pay ransoms more easily. Even though kidnapping for ransom is a high risk endeavor, most amateurs will try anyway. The thrill of a big time score from a well known or wealthy victim provides a ton of temptation.

WEALTH IS OK, BUT FAME IS DANGEROUS

There is no easier way to acquire fame than to kill somebody who is already famous. If, in addition to becoming rich you also become well known, BE CAREFUL. Famous people are murdered often---just so the murderer can gain fame.

MAINTAIN A LOW PROFILE.

Learn from the Panama Canal. It manages two unequal levels of ocean water with a <u>series of locks</u>. As a wealthy person, you have elevated your water level, and those beneath you will constantly and forever seek your runoff. Lock down not only your possessions, but hide the information about those locks and the wealth behind them.

As long as you remain with your upper level friends, you'll be OK. Most victims I've interviewed ventured through the canal to the lower water level. They went for great chinese food at a converted warehouse in the barrio section of town. They visited a porn shop or a well known hooker hangout and parked their car in an alley where nobody would notice them. One man I interviewed parked his car in Los Angeles near 6th and Spring streets because he could get terrific discounts on shirts. Daylight, but still . . .

Don't dress flamboyantly in poor places. Don't park your expensive car in poor neighborhoods. All financial records stay hidden, perhaps on a cheap computer not connected to the internet, and coded for password-only entry.

Be extremely careful about who comes into your private space. Most low income employees can easily be persuaded to gather information about you. Don't give money to pan handlers in a bad neighborhood. They look into your wallet and signal muggers.

Recently I did some work for a wealthy couple who hired a housekeeper with a license plate frame which read: "Don't like my driving? Dial 1-800-EAT-CRAP." I'm sure the housekeeper had some boy friends or acquaintances who were all too eager to know any private details about her wealthy employers.

RUN BACKGROUND CHECKS ON EVERYONE YOU HIRE

Here's the general rule. All employees fill out a complete

application and you verify date of birth and social security number. Relatives, next of kin, and other vital information is important.

PAYING EMPLOYEES

Your checks (**never cash**) need to show the dates for which compensation was paid. On the back of the check write this: *Paid and accepted by the payee as full payment.* His or her signature goes right under that written statement and pretty much precludes a later demand for wages already paid. The front side of your checks should show no name, no address, no phone number and **absolutely no social security number.** That will keep you from using the checks for shopping, which is an absolute no-no. It also saves your identity from publication by TelChek which picks up all of that information from each and every check a merchant receives and publishes that information freely.

ATTACK---YOURSELF.

As soon as you're wealthy, you must attack yourself. Hire---perhaps a knowledgeable friend, an off-duty police officer or a private security agency to break into your house. Give him an instruction letter and have him fax the local police department before he does the following: Set up an armed robbery using his index finger as a weapon, see if he could kidnap your child, car jack you in your driveway, abduct your wife, or rob your business. The U.S. military is not stupid and rather well prepared---because they play war games. You need to do the same.

The discovery of weaknesses and defects in your defense system may very well save many times over what you invest. Besides that, it will improve your own chances survival and perhaps, save your life.

What about your schedules? Have you become Mrs Routine so that any abductor could predict where you would be the same time tomorrow?

The richer you become, the more attractive target you are. Increase your defenses as your wealth piles up. That way, you will probably save yourself, your loved ones and your peace of mind.

Security during travel follows cost. Planes are relatively safe. Trains are more dangerous. Busses are the worst. During a Greyhound strike, several rifle ambushes persuaded drivers to stay at home and "leave the driving" to union negotiators.

Several line-ups by local police of bus passengers have yielded lots of drugs and all kinds of weapons.

I personally visited a bus depot and surveyed my fellow travelers. Scary!

Chapter 8

TRAVEL

FIRST! CONSIDER DESTINATION

I went personally to the Hawaii State Visitors and Convention Bureau on Oahu and interviewed Sandra Fukushima. Hawaii issues video tapes showing island scenery and a variety of activities. Is that the lure? I asked, "What is the main reason people should visit Hawaii?" She answered, "Spirit of ALOHA."

All around you see cards defining the acronym. The first word, *Akahai,* means KINDNESS to be expressed with TENDERNESS. I don't get that same feeling in many foreign countries I've visited, even though I speak the languages.

So the moral of the comparison is this: Go some place where the people are kind, crime is low, a good spirit prevails, the climate is decent, and the air and water are pure.

Not all Hawaiian Islands are absolutely safe. Oahu has some crime and certain areas can be dangerous. On Kaua'i where I live, the main feature: Cops who are not very busy and lots of pickup trucks are parked with unsecured goods lying in their beds. People there respect the property of others.

THIRD WORLD BARGAINS

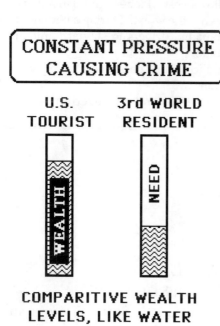

CONSTANT PRESSURE
CAUSING CRIME

U.S.
TOURIST

3rd WORLD
RESIDENT

WEALTH

NEED

COMPARITIVE WEALTH
LEVELS, LIKE WATER

I've visited all of Europe, Costa Rica, Mexico, (speak fluent spanish) Fiji, Australia, New Zealand (super place) and discovered this: If the people are poor, (right) and you are rich by comparison (left) then the pressure to commit a crime is intense unless there is a common ethic (religious faith) that inhibits criminal activity. When I lived in Bangkok, Thailand, for example, guards with Machetes guarded the entrance to my high rise on Sukhumvit. "Thieves Market" was a commonly accepted place to buy stolen goods.

So---plan your vacation carefully. Ask somebody who has been there. How? Get a reference number from a travel agent. Remember---the general rule about human behavior is that morals go down hill. Then, as soon as you arrive anywhere, visit a beauty parlor and get your hair done. Beauticians tell everything!

Incidentally, prepare individual head shots of each family member **half toned** and carry these to the foreign country. You may need lots of pictures of someone, especially a child who is lost. Glossy photos will not copy on a machine. Half tones will.

> SAVE MONEY WITH A FOREIGN AIRLINE?
> Fly Saudi Airlines in the middle East. Pass by security guards
> who earn less than U.S. minimum wage. It's called, Air Chance. Hi-
> jackers can ruin your whole day.

GETTING THERE

On public transportation, the frequency of crime goes down as cost of travel increases. Bus and train stations get bums and weirdoes. Buses carry some human animals you can't believe. One police search of an interstate bus recently yielded several weapons and enough drugs to fill a briefcase. On the other hand, you can be pretty sure you won't encounter a weapon on an airplane. As a general rule, cheap travel puts you personally at risk; expensive travel puts only your property at risk.

Another factor is the crowds. With a lot of people around, crimes against persons don't occur as often. But you have to watch out for your property. If they can grab your purse or your bag, they'll disappear into the crowd and be difficult to chase.

Overall, the same defense principles you apply elsewhere apply when traveling. Avoiding crime in transit is much the same as avoiding crime anywhere—-with a few new variations on the theme.

In most tourist areas, criminals can steal property without much fear of prosecution. Hawaiian car rental agencies will tell you to leave your car empty with the trunk open and carry everything on your person. Why? Because thieves will break open the trunk and damage the car beyond the value of the goods they steal. Car burglary against tourists anywhere is profitable. Even if the criminal gets caught, the victim doesn't want to fly back from home to testify after his vacation. So—-tourists should be most concerned about theft. Who steals? All kinds of people, although low class, rough looking transients will be prime suspects. They frequently have a drug crazy need for more money than a well paid executive can make. Women with the same needs get cash in other ways, but they can also be thieves when employed as maids, clerks in hotels, etc. If you travel cheaply, then you can expect the employees of the firms you'll be dealing with to be in a lower economic bracket. Guard your goods; dress down to the level of your traveling companions; don't flash any money or jewelry. In a motel, use the safe or vault. Failing, that, get creative in the art of hiding valuables.

Once you understand that danger levels change as your modes of transportation change, consider some of the different ways in which you may be traveling. Then, make crime defense plans accordingly.

ON FOOT

If you walk much and your neighborhood is rough, don't carry valuables; carry defensive weapons. Purses attract thieves like sticky paper attracts flies. Walk against traffic. In Los Angeles one of the month's 263 violent fatalities was a 94 year old grandmother with $8 in her purse which she had looped around her wrist. Purse snatchers came from behind in a car and dragged her 100 feet to her death.

Day or night, don't walk on the right side of the road. Even if up on a sidewalk, walk on the left---**against** traffic. Also, walk against the arrows in a parking lot. Purse snatchers drive slowly behind women walking in the same direction as parking lot traffic. The passenger leans out of the car---and your purse is gone.

If the neighborhood is bad (many U.S. cities) walk in the street. Too many people have been assaulted by drunks in doorways, muggers in alleys, etc. Seldom will they come all the

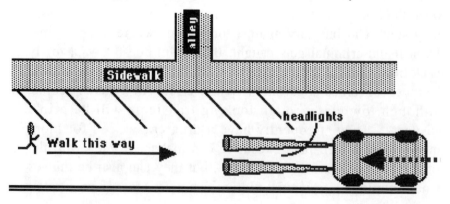

way out into the street to bother you. In addition to the above, stay on main streets. At night, don't travel where it's dark. Street hoodlums normally shoot out street lights so they have more freedom---less identity.

Dress for combat more than looks. You can fight freely and run fast in tennis shoes and loose-fitting pants. Tight skirts and high heels leave you at a disadvantage.

Don't walk or ride around alone. Many street criminals work in pairs. They have more nerve that way. Besides that, they're afraid of losing. Seldom will they attack a superior number. So two or three in your group are less likely to be attacked than one alone.

When bodyguards work a detail, each has an area of responsibility. You too. One of you watches the right and rear, from 2 - 8 on your defense clock. The other scans the front, from 7 - 3. To be professional, overlap.

Another great advantage to traveling in pairs is this: Broader range of weaponry. One carries short range weapons, the other carries long range. One carries gas, the other carries firepower. Warn each other about danger.

Notice that rowdy group a block away moving

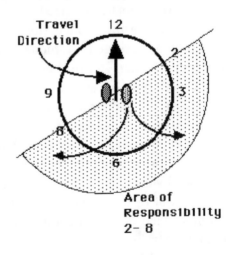

WALKING IN PAIRS
AREAS OF RESPONSIBILITY

Travel Direction   12

9

3

8

6

Area of Responsibility
2- 8

Always---12 o'clock is straight ahead. Person on the right scans from two thru eight---the rear area. Talk to each other---eliminate surprises.

towards you? Walk across the street or into an occupied building. Don't stare at them. When you can't avoid such a group, approach with your head up and seek eye contact with one member of the group. Remain calm. Do not display fear but at the same time don't create a challenge that might require a response from them. "Dissin" is street talk for disrespect, and you would be surprised at how little it takes to incite a gang attack, especially when you're alone.

In crowded areas, such as parades, Mardi Gras, sports events, block pickpockets by sewing Velcro on your pockets. When a pickpocket lifts the flap, the ripping noise tells you what happened, and also lets him know he has been announced.

In transit, from bus to airport, van to bus station, etc. don't allow anyone not in porter's uniform to handle your baggage. If a stranger does handle your bags, chances are he'll run with them or extort a tremendous fee for carrying.

WHILE SLEEPING IN A HOTEL

To eliminate the need for using elevators or stairwells at night, sleep on the ground floor. Take **NO CALLS!** Put your phone on a message-only mode. Thus it's difficult for anyone to find out whether you're there or not. **NOBODY** maintains the room while you occupy it. Anyone can buy a pair of coveralls. They then enter the motel, pick up a house phone and fish until some unsuspecting person in her room bites---by allowing the robber in coveralls in to fix something. Result: Robbery, etc.

Improve security by staying in the room while it's being serviced by cleaning staff. Keep expensive cameras, watches, and jewelry out of sight whenever hotel staff are in the room. Place room service dishes outside your room and thus eliminate one more reason for staff to enter. With duct tape and plastic baggies, stick valuables to the under sides of desks, drawers or other furniture. Otherwise, use the hotel's safe.

Keep the security latch or chain on at all times. Leave the "Do Not Disturb" sign on the outside of the door. Close curtains

> The DO NOT DISTURB sign I hang on the outside door knob helps me to feel cozy because it helps to keep the hotel room looking like home---a dump.

on the entrance wall, especially when absent. Leave a TV or radio talk show station on when you leave. Do all of the above, and your motel stay should be reasonably safe.

SLEEPING ON THE GO

If you sleep while traveling on a bus, ferry, etc., sneak a secure line (parachute cord) to your pack or briefcase where nobody can see it; then tie that line off where a slight tug on it will wake you but a hard yank won't throw you off balance. Use a coin locker if you'll be spending several hours in an airport or train station. But then park your carcass where you can keep an eye on your locker. Lots of coin lockers are ripped off by people who rent the locker, then make a copy of the key.

When sleeping on planes and trains, keep tickets and other valuables in your inside coat pocket. Place your carry-on bag under the seat in front of you and put your feet on the bag while you sleep. With shoes off, you'll be much more sensitive to any movement.

AIRPORTS, BUS AND TRAIN STATIONS

Women, keep your checks and tickets in a handbag or briefcase. Shoulder bags with heavy straps make a lot of sense for the female traveler. They make it difficult for a thief to grab your bag and run. Wear the bag over your shoulder, then cover it with a coat so it can't be seen.

Form an alliance if you're alone. Just be certain the person you pick is reliable. Choose women over men, clean over dirty, well-dressed over shabby and age over youth. Until recently, women and crime didn't normally mix; well dressed frequently portrayed earnings, and older people grew up in a an atmosphere of high moral character.

Recently, I flew from Hawaii to LA. then took a van downtown to catch a Greyhound bus into the desert. I was pass-out tired, and my bus wouldn't leave for two and a half hours. I saw two teenage girls with bags huddled in the corner, more scared than I. In a quick interview, I learned they were from England. They'd come here to be nannies at a children's camp, saved their money, and were touring through the USA. I needed rest so I said, "Let's make a deal. I'll plop down here and sleep; you watch my bags and warn me if a problem develops. Tell anybody who comes around that I just got out of the mental hospital in Camarillo and they should be extra quiet. If they bother either of you girls, I'll take them apart." The girls were wide-eyed and more than happy to stand watch. I rigged a line from my backpack to my belt loop and covered it. My tote bag was my pillow. We moved to a strategic corner, and I slept well.

The same general plan works in youth hostels, air terminals, on ferries etc. Do a little interview work and find someone you can trust to team up with. Then take turns sleeping and guarding.

Wear your helmet! Drivers on drugs don't see a cyclist, they see a bike that will get them a quick fix for just nudging you with their cars. Also, you can duck your head and thus block a lot of incoming blows during a hand-to-hand argument.

Hospital Air Transport helicopter pilot Ben Springer of Washington State warns: "I've transported several cases in which the accident was small, but the head trauma was tremendous."

ON A BIKE

I took a bike ride around San Diego recently. I was a cop there and I know the city pretty well. From homeless people, I learned things are tough. Homeless people trash the tennis courts through the fence during daylight matches. Drugs abound. Car burglary is common. Night times are dangerous.

In many large cities, you could pedal to a store in daylight, leave your bike without locking it, then kiss it good-bye. You can tell how many are stolen by the street price of a 10-speed: Under $15. Bike riders not only need to watch their wheels; they need to take care of themselves. In a pinch without any other weapon, your bike pump used as a pool-cue penetrator or a club will give you *some* help, at least.

If you ride alone, you can take your mountain bike into the wilderness and be fairly safe from crime---unless you ride where marijuana is being cultivated... You can disappear into the woods, and nobody knows you're there unless you make a lot of noise or burn a smoky fire. You can also ride with a group and enjoy safety in numbers. But if you ride alone and travel down streets in a bad part of town or on a secluded bike path in a city park, watch your bottom. Ambush is a distinct possibility. One sideways shove and you're down. Anything more and you may not get up.

When I lived in Oregon, I used to ride the logging roads of Lobster Valley and I always carried good firepower because of the pot growers in the area. There, however, I had a chance because I was alone on the roads most of the time and could hear or see trouble. In city parks, it's not like that. One rider in Balboa park passed a bush and a homeless guy came from nowhere and hit him from the side and then took money from him while he was down. He identified the man and the police caught him. A month or so later, the same guy was back in the park.

Ride the way you walk—-against traffic. You can't afford to get hit from behind. On a country road, you can always ditch. In a city, you go up on the sidewalk or pull in between parked cars and halt.

When you ride against traffic, watch out at driveways and corners! Drivers <u>emerging from the side</u> will be looking for <u>oncoming</u> traffic from the opposite direction only.

TAKING CABS

Never get in a cab unless you first ask how much the fare is. In the Philippines, the answer for fare to Clark Air Force Base was, "Oh, it's a short trip, you can pay me what you want." Then, after we arrived, fifteen Filipinos surrounded my cab while the driver tried to extort big bucks from me. I lost money rather than donate blood to the gang.

In Spain once, the cab driver told me, "Whatever the meter says." He then proceeded to make more than four right turns so the shadows were back on the same side as they were when we started. (See Paul's *Never Get Lost.*) I got out of that cab, paid the driver, and caught another taxi.

When taking a cab alone in a foreign country, sit directly behind the driver. Order him to lock all the doors. In the Philippines and Mexico, drivers often go to a place where they meet a gang of twenty. Routinely, when I worked as a cop on the Tijuana border, we would see beaten sailors dumped back at the border in skivvies only. In Thailand, I traveled with a Green Beret buddy who always sat behind the driver. One day a cab driver made a wrong turn into a dark and cruddy section of town, but a very sharp 2" pen knife caused the driver to stop, back it up, and drive in a new direction. Later, my buddy had the driver stop in front of a cop; he got out and paid for the ride in plain sight. It was a polite encounter.

ON THE BUS

This is now a dangerous way to travel in the U.S. I always wonder about the drivers---they look so respectable. But they settled a recent strike by using snipers to pepper the buses with rifle fire from overhead bridges. Bus travel is cheap, which may be why the terminals are human junk yards. Some of the travelers scare me. On a bus, feel free to change your seat as the situation demands. Pick clean looking seating companions and sit where a crowd has gathered. Remember---safety in numbers.

Bus and train terminals see lots of scams. Most have to do with ticket exchanges. Don't buy tickets from anyone but the airlines or rail ticket office. A popular scam works like this: A presentable-looking individual will approach you and explain that his or her wallet or purse has been stolen along with his tickets. They have a Rolex or Nikon or something worth a great deal more than the cost of the ticket they need. If you're willing to buy them a ticket, they will give you the "item" for security. When they get home they will send you the money for the ticket plus $100 and you can return their property. Sure. . Either the property is junk, stolen, or it's a fake.

Generally, keep your distance from strangers. Don't let them lead you into a conversation. Get tactically situated if you have to wait. Seats against a wall or in corners are best. If you're waiting in a long line and someone scary gets behind you, address the situation. Say, "Are you waiting to buy a ticket?" If the answer is yes, say, "Go ahead of me, please. My bus won't be leaving for a long time." You need to stand <u>behind</u> a suspicious person, <u>not in front</u> of him.

With luggage in the overhead rack, you'd best stay awake. If you're really tired, move your bags to a window seat, then sleep leaning up against them from an aisle seat.

In a foreign country, buses and trains are somewhat safer. Even so, I make an alliance with somebody before I sleep. I once took my 10-year old son on a train trip deep in Mexico through the Tarajumara Indian country. I speak fluent Spanish and made friends with a *Cabo* (corporal) in the *federales*. I taught him a few things about his German assault rifle. He taught me a few things about the absolute authority he had to shoot any suspect. We slept in shifts and I never lost a dime.

A NOTE ON FOREIGN TRAVEL

Assuming the purpose of travel is pleasure, why not go somewhere nice—-where you don't have to worry about crime? What parts of the world are most crime-free? As it happens, English is spoken there. New Zealand is a country with a tradition of peace, friendliness and propriety. In Australia, I stayed in a rough neighborhood and found it free of crime. Parts of Canada are also nice—-notably Vancouver Island, B.C., which is full of people who are lovely to the core. I lost my wallet on a bus there. Someone found it, turned it in, and the BC Transit people called me. They returned it with the hundred dollars and all credit cards untouched. On the other hand, some Canadian cities are now a little rough. Although I love Hawaii and live there, it isn't crime free. Parts of Oahu are downright dangerous. If you want to experience the feeling of a lone black person at a white country club in the South, try to surf with Hawaiian locals on their beach. You're a haole, and they may bruise you.

Europe has its fair share of crime. Besides, you have to hassle with the petty crooks who take advantage of the fact that you can't speak the language. In Germany, for example, a hotel added a good-sized surcharge to a bill for bathing. They claimed my father took 9 baths per day and charged him for it. In Italy, once, a 16 year old sweetheart of a girl shortchanged me and I caught her at it. *"Mire,"* I said, as I held the coin up, *"Cinque, cinque."* (Look, five, five!) Oh—-she was so embarrassed. She took back my coin and gave me some others, which I dumped in my pocket. "Got to get up real early to fool me," I thought. Later, after I'd left the cafeteria, I recounted the money; she'd shortchanged me worse the second time.

Mexico crime is near intolerable. News reports of over 500 violent crimes a day in Mexico City are an understatement. Cops who attend the academy take a class in how to solicit a bribe. One recent homicide incident involved cops who killed a tourist and used his ATM card.

In Fussa, South of Tokyo, Japan, whole racks of bikes outside a department stood without locks. The crime rate there was low. However, in Guatamala recently I went into a bank and noticed a guard with a machine gun. I spoke to him and asked why he was armed that heavily. *"Hay muchos ladrones,* (There are many thieves.) he said. He wore a bullet proof vest, too. Likewise, when you see broken glass or barbed wire on the top of a wall, the criminal germs in the neighborhood are restless. Be on guard.

If you want to see some real crime, visit Washington D.C. or several other large U.S. cities. I called D.C. and told them I was former FBI agent and asked, "Could I carry a gun in your city?"

"Definitely not," she answered.

"Who made that law?" I asked.

"City council."

Funny---no guns allowed, but you can sit on a porch near the White House on <u>any given night</u> and hear sporadic gunfire.

Also, don't spend time in St. Croix, U.S. Virgin Islands, where, after Hurricane Hugo, even the police and National Guard were looting. The crime rate has been astronomical ever since.

IN THE AIR

Air travel offers fewer problems than cheaper forms of transportation. Not only do you mix 'n mingle with a higher class of passenger, but inspections make theft less easy. Carry on as much baggage as you can. Baggage handlers are poorly paid employees who sometimes supplement their income. For check in, I use cheap luggage in which I keep a candle. Drop a little hot candle wax to make a seal on your baggage locks and you'll be able to tell if the bag was opened since you saw it last. Another way, either pull a hair from your head or a match out of a matchbook. Hang one of these half in and out of the case so they barely protrude when closed. If it's gone when you land, your luggage was opened.

Overstuffed luggage is frequently dropped by handlers because they know it will pop open so they can pilfer. Put an ID tag (no home address) inside your luggage. People who steal luggage around airports often cut outside ID tags off. You can identify your bags with your ID hidden inside.

In the terminal, use the dining and rest room facilities located inside the security check points. Crime is less prevalent there. Board the plane early while the overhead storage is empty. Store your carry-ons directly over your seat; otherwise they may be gone when you land. Be careful about what you put in the overhead storage compartments. Someone could grab your stuff while pretending to get something out of their own gear.

> I heard they recently found Amelia Erhardt. She is quoted as saying, "Don't worry about me, but please find my luggage."

Put spare toothbrush and paste, a razor, and one clean change of clothes in your carry-on baggage in case your checked-in bags get sent by mistake to Egypt. It happens all the time.

ON THE BEACHES

Buy a beach towel with a matching hand towel. Then, sew the two together so the smaller towel makes a color blend-in pocket with Velcro flap on the big towel. Carry your beach goodies in there. With the pocket on the sandy side, nobody will see it. Even if you have to go for your gun because you suspect trouble, it will look as if you're wiping your hands. If the trouble really develops, don't display the pistol; just shoot a hole right through the terry cloth. Remember, the gun trick won't be a good idea in most foreign countries. Get caught with a *pistola* in Mexico, for example, and you will either have to pay a healthy bribe or spend time rotting in a Mexican prison.

A knife will do the same trick but it has to be sharp. Razor sharp. Have it sharpened by a professional in a knife shop.

Hollywood stunt woman Sunny Woods has spent more time on the beach than most other humans spend at work. Most of her life she was single and therefore, on her own. On the beach she carries her car keys, money, ID, and a loaded pistol. Even though she goes swimming a lot, she hasn't lost anything. Why? She looks around, and when nobody is watching, she buries it all a few inches below the surface in a plastic baggie. Casually, she rolls over on her towel. Then she gets up, goes into the water, and returns to the towel. After she dries off, she rolls over, sits up, and digs the baggie out. With a handgun in the towel pocket, she's secure on secluded beaches.

Two obnoxious men on two separate occasions have come close to meeting Jesus at judgement when they

TWO MATCHING TOWELS SEWN

bothered her. But there is a sixth sense in every criminal that tells them——pressing this is probably a bad idea. Maybe it's the way she spoke when she knew she had a gun under the towel. Perhaps it was her posture——or the way she held her head. The guys left.

GENERAL RULES

When traveling, never carry more cash than necessary. Of course, make sure to have enough cash to satisfy a mugger who might lose his temper if you carry nothing. Carry traveler's checks and use credit cards you can replace. Your responsibility for charges on the cards ends as soon as you report them stolen. You would think that's good news, but it's the opposite.

Not long ago I flew to New Orleans with a Louisiana sheriff who told me victims in the French Quarter were being robbed at gun point, then shot. The police couldn't figure out why. It's because dead victims can't report their cards stolen. Fences will pay a higher price because they can charge on the cards for a longer time. You can fix this for under $1. Toss all your important documents (licenses, ID's phone calling cards) and credit cards on a copier and push the button. Copy both sides. Staple the sheets together. Leave that list at home along with your list of traveler's checks serial numbers, and the serial numbers of any computers, cameras, guns etc. If you don't report in on time, have someone at home cancel your cards and inform the local police of the card and I.D. numbers. That should help lead to your killer. It *might* also save your life when you explain that the canceling procedure is automatic if you don't show up tomorrow.

Never discuss your vacation or business plans with hotel staff or any other local. Many hotel employees drink in local bars and may have a moonlight job as an information peddler on commission. You draw attention to yourself by either over tipping or not tipping at all. If you don't tip enough, you become a subject of sore discussion about how rich and stingy you are. Tip too much, and they talk about what a rich, big spender you were. Either way, you may become a target. Just tip fairly.

When planning your travels, do a little research on the local laws about weapons and defense. This is doubly important when you're visiting a foreign country. Most officials get awfully upset about an undocumented firearm.

Learn to depend on other defense measures when you can't carry a handgun. You can almost always carry a knife. Check it in at airports and you retrieve it when you land. Make sure yours opens with one hand. (See Don's *Everybody's Knife Bible.*) You can also make a Bo or a short club with the clothes rack bar out of your hotel room when you go jogging. With a saw blade or knife, you can make a decent weapon out of any broom. Roll the handle and tap on the back of a knife blade to knock it progressively into the wood to achieve a clean cut.

Illustration above taken from *Everybody's Knife Bible.* Tapping on the back of the blade will almost give you a square cut. Go through a broom handle this way, then point the ends. Use this as a Bo if you have to walk in a dangerous area.

Be aware of everything going on around you all the time. Observe, then assess, then make decisions about plans. Train yourself to look for something out of place. Is someone acting strange or nervous?

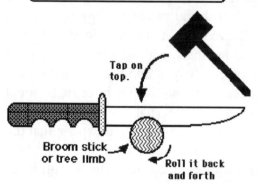

CUTTING THROUGH WOOD EVENLY

Tap on top.

Broom stick or tree limb

Roll it back and forth

Long coats worn in hot summer times can mean weapons concealed underneath. Look at the pictures of criminals on TV and in newspapers. Ladies walking in shopping malls during the day often make statements of beauty, elegance and wealth. Notice how criminals dress to make a statement of their own: Hellacious tatoos, chains and studded wrist leather all indicate this person belongs to a sub-culture with different values from your own.

That doesn't mean crime can't come from a well-groomed man, but when a person makes an out of line statement, it generally gives evidence of an abused, born-for-welfare-only, bastard child who needs desperately to compensate for inadequacy. My advice: Assess the potential harm, plan for defense.

Think about what you can do if a violent situation develops. Don't walk into a trap. Avoid trouble. You're a good bodyguard when you <u>keep</u> out of trouble. Former cops and Karate pros are not as good at body guarding because they focus on <u>getting</u> out of trouble, then making an arrest. That's how they think. But I want you to think way ahead of that---stay trouble free always.

ON A DATE

SHOULD WE BE ANGRY WITH EMILY---POST?

I take some real issue with Emily Post. People who were trying to be polite have caused permanent damage to many women and death to others. What is this book teaching!

Ladies go first---right into a robber's arms as they leave or enter an elevator, walk into a trap as the gentleman holds the door for her, etc. Men walk on the street side, so the lady gets attacked from an alley. That's not to blame the writer, however. It's just that times have changed. If you want to be a **real** gentleman, be a bodyguard and step into danger first. Don't send the lady.

Men, quit driving. Let the woman drive and you ride shotgun. Be a LIFO man; forget Emily Post until she learns what's right for the "great society" Lyndon Johnson created. LIFO then tells you how to load into your car. Opposite procedure for elevator, parking lot, dark alley, etc. and it means Last In, First Out. If you get into trouble, she should leave. Once out of harm's way, perhaps a block or so, she can call police, honk the horn, flash lights and try to get some help. A shot from a gun, even in the air, will cause many perps to panic and flee.

AT CROWDED PUBLIC EVENTS

Be careful in a crowd. Your wallet goes in your front pocket. Carry only a little cash, your tickets, and I.D. Credit card? Carry it in a jacket liner or stuffed down in your socks.

> **DON'T!** DO NOT carry a credit card in a foreign country with a large limit. If you must, get an additional card with a low limit. In some cases, (Mexico City) people have been kidnapped and held until the card goes over limit.

Ladies, use fanny packs. Don't wear jewelry; blend in with the crowd. Don't wear anything or do anything which might draw the attention of thieves.

As crime becomes more prevalent, travel is more risk-laden. Still, though, you may have to go somewhere to do something you can't do through the mail or over the phone. Apply the precautions and tricks in this chapter, and your chances of having a safe and enjoyable trip will be much improved.

CONVICT---LOSS OF RIGHT TO SUE

Why do convicted felons have a right to sue anyone? Conviction for a crime automatically has to wipe out the criminal's standing to litigate. Convicts have abused the privilege. They break in, beat up, rob, and rape their victims. If they get hurt in the process, they sue their victims from jail. They get a free law library along with all the time in the world to sue anyone for anything. Meanwhile, it robs the victim's peace of mind, costs attorneys fees to defend, lessens the victim's ability to earn his own livelihood and return to a normal, post-trauma life. In general, it makes a mockery of our justice system.

Even if he loses the lawsuit, the convict plaintiff becomes a hero in prison. His litigation sends a message to all U.S. law-abiding citizens: "Don't disturb a burglar in your home; it may be less trouble to let him take it all."

Is there a politician out there who can fix this?

Some believe that the allure of a woman is what arouses rapists. Not so.

Good looking women are less at risk because their looks intimidate. I interviewed a model who dressed in a bikini at a motorcycle show. She said, "Some of the men who photographed me were bikers in colors and they shaking so severely they couldn't hold the camera steady."

Most rapists are low-self-esteem, insecure men who have a need to compensate by conquering a woman and taking "love" on command against her will.

"In my country, over 2,000 rapes occur every day."

Source: ABC News.

Chapter 8

SPECIAL FOR WOMEN: DEFEND AGAINST FORCIBLE RAPE BY A STRANGER

If you want to recover **after** a rape, call a rape crisis center. They're everywhere and they've had a lot of experience. They tell me that in most states now, you're entitled by law to an advocate in post-rape procedure. Knowledgeable and highly competent counselors are available to help you with trauma. None of the above is my area; I believe you can avoid being a victim **before** and conquer a rapist **during** any atack.

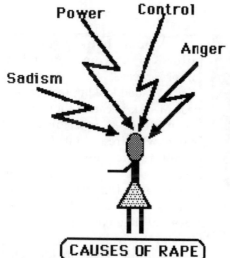

Power   Control

Anger

Sadism

CAUSES OF RAPE

Sexual gratification is **not** the goal of the rapist. He needs to take "love" in the presence of pain and hatred. A display of fear turns him on. A display of anger and hate turns him off.

FORCIBLE RAPE COMMITTED BY A STRANGER

In 99' the Spanish Newspaper of Los Angeles, *LA OPINION,* reported that forcible rape represented only 18% of all rapes reported. I believe it's much higher. As a matter of fact, your chances of actually being raped are one out of three during your lifetime. Maybe one out of two, or 50%. Nobody knows. Why? Not all rapes are reported. That's understandable. When researching, I talked to rape counselors; I couldn't bear to talk with victims. They'd suffered a terrible crime; it's ignominious beyond description. It assaulted their psyche so severely that some blocked out the memory. Many never got over the trauma.

To write a book like this, you have to find out first how criminals operate and what motivates them. So I sat there with the rapist and listened intently. He described how he was pulling her hair and banging her head against the wall during the act. "Yeah," I nodded. To get the material, I had to be with him in the moment as if I too were enjoying the process. After that, I interviewed some of the rape crisis counselors and got in touch with victim's feelings, I had personal problems. It was horrible beyond description. All criminals take something from their victims. Robbers and burglars steal possessions. Murderers steal life. Rapists steal dignity and self esteem, which forces their victims to live the rest of their lives feeling degraded, scared, trashed and worthless.

THE MIND SET OF THE RAPIST?

In all the crimes I've analyzed, I find commonality in the perpetrators. No matter what the offense or the M.O. (Modus Operendi---Latin for the way in which a criminal operates in each crime) the bad guys come to a low place in their lives where there is a compulsion to prevail, conquer, get over on, or put someone else down. Gamblers are somewhat the same. The excitement of risking money on a horse and winning becomes a compulsion.

> ### THE PSYCHOLOGICAL ATMOSPHERE IN RAPE
> Your unfriendly rapist wants---needs---your shyness and fear in order to make his arousal function.
> Your job is to manage the interlude so that he feels the opposite. A shrill voice, hate, anger, boldness and arrogance all go to destroy the psychological atmosphere he needs. Take charge. Talk to him as if he were a bad dog. Punish him---verbally and physically to make him flee and choose a different victim.

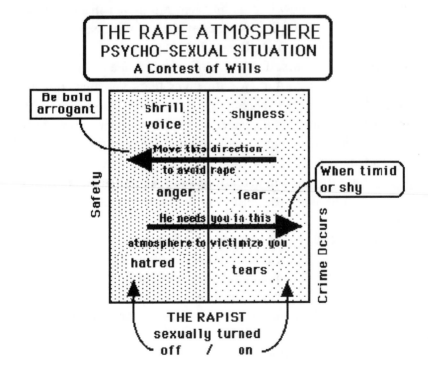

Burglars speak about real rush of excitement that comes from breaking into someone else's house and stealing from them. The more clever they are, the better it makes them feel. Even when in prison, the common thread in convicts is their desire to "get over on the man." If they can escape, they win the adulation of all their peers and experience what to them is the the ultimate victory.

Rapists are no different. All they want to do is conquer a woman. One Los Angeles sheriff who caught a serial rapist analyzed a map and figured out that the perpetrator probably lived near the neighborhood where most of the rapes occurred. So he reviewed all the neighborhood field interrogations from regular patrol officers who stopped suspicious males at odd hours. After he caught the rapist, he searched his apartment and found photos of this guy with all kinds of willing women. Lack of sex was not a problem. His compulsion to rape was so strong that it made him feel great when he had absolutely conquered and prevailed over a victim. No matter how bad he hurt her, raping her made him feel loved and gratified in spite of what he thought of himself.

YOUR SOLUTION

Now ask yourself, what kind of man needs to get even, overcome, conquer? A man with inner fears and inadequacies. How could you turn the tables on such a man? Cause him to feel those inner fears and inadequacies all over again. He's looking for the satisfaction that comes with creating submission. To avoid being raped, you give him the opposite. It's as if you and the rapist enter into an arm wrestling contest. Instead of limply allowing him to slam your arm into the table, you strike first and slam his.

Where does rape occur most frequently?

1. In the home. Attacker hides in home or garage and surprises you. The majority of rapes occur here.

2. In a car. Surprise in a parking lot or dimly lit street. Possible abduction to a secluded area where further crimes occur.

3. Outdoors. Parks. Rapists hide in bushes and

attack weaponless joggers who're running alone. After dark, early mornings are most frequent times.

This is a battle you can win by making the first attack. Don't wait for him to molest you. Win the psychological battle by making the first verbal assault.

If alone, you're an easier target. As much as you can, go everywhere in pairs. If you don't carpool to work, use a dummy in the passenger seat.

OPPOSING FORCES IN A RAPE

I define public elevators as human traps which move vertically between places where no help is available. Remember the thrill seeking mind of the man who needs to get over on the world. Wouldn't he just have the best time if he raped you in an elevator stopped between floors where crowds were close but nobody could help you? When alone, avoid elevators and use the stairs so you have room to retreat, counter attack or escape.

USING THE DEFCON SYSTEM

Situation: You notice a man leering at you from a distance and he looks mighty unfriendly. Quickly look behind you. Robbers work in pairs, but rapists work alone.

In no other case is the Defense Condition analysis system so helpful as in the case of rape by a stranger. At DefCon #1, when a threat is 10 ft. away, you should access your weapon or look around for a weapon you can improvise, do a quick search

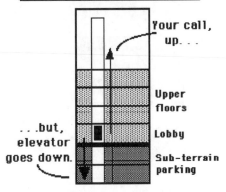

ELEVATORS PROGRAMMED TO ASSIST CRIMINALS IN THE BASEMENTS

Your call, up. . .

Upper floors

Lobby

Sub-terrain parking

. . .but, elevator goes down.

ELEVATORS ARE: Small cells travelling up or down in which no help is available. Take stairs.

103

for a means of escape, seek out a place or people where help is available, or search for a place where defense will be easier. If it's a stare in your direction you don't like, stare back angrily, defiantly, with the meanest look you can give.

Don't look away, slouch, or act afraid. This is particularly important. A mean look directly into the eyes of the man you fear does two things for you. 1. It makes him feel identified. 2. It tells him you are the kind of woman he wants to avoid. On the other hand, a timid look or averted eyes send this signal, "Please leave me alone; I'm afraid." To the rapist, such a message incites sexual arousal which comes from a feeling of power and power is measurable. It's the psychological distance between machismo and weakness.

At <u>DefCon #2</u>, your weapon should be pointed (under cover) at your suspect with the safety off. Also, you should be moving to safer, perhaps higher, ground. If you can retreat and get away, do that. If you get verbal contact, put it down right away. Talk to the suspect in the same tone of voice you would use on a dog. Commands such as, *"Get away from me, now! Stay where you are! Get out of here!"* all serve to overpower the rapist and destroy his machismo. He wanted to control and hurt you. When you treat him coldly and command him, you rise above him and he no longer looks down on you as a victim. If you appear to be weak, shy

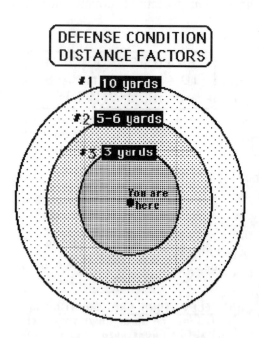

DEFENSE CONDITION
DISTANCE FACTORS

#1 10 yards

#2 5-6 yards

#3 3 yards

You are here

or fearful, you attract him and he becomes aroused. That's why rape defense classes teach you posture, <u>head up, shoulders back</u>

> Women: Turn with your back to a mirror and bring your hands up high enough to bend your arm to its max. Now look at your elbows. Are they sharp and pointed? Many are, and if so, this is a great in- close move for you.

<u>and purposeful</u> ways of walking. Take charge and stay in charge. This is a great time to let any anger you have about anything come to the surface.

Finally, <u>DefCon #3.</u> The threat is close. Note here, of course, that all threats don't sneak up on you in three stages. Most rapists are good at surprise and ambush. They have plenty of time to study the area, and stalking you is pleasurable because they perceive you as helpless and in their power, (even though you may not know it). Strangers who rape often catch their victims off guard by surprise. If you're accosted, you'll have to defend. The shrillest, most demeaning tone of voice is what you need. If you have it in you, it's time to become 100% bitch.

Once you've screamed insults at this person and he keeps coming on, you have a real reason to fear for your life. Rape is a long term threat to both your mental and physical health. Once you're afraid for your life, you can take his life in self defense. If you have a weapon, it's reasonable to believe that you were so afraid that you fired several times. Therefore, lethal force is right, as well as righteous

> This is a great move for women because long fingernails are a natural for a rapist's eyes. Don't just jab. Drive the thumbs in deep and leave them there as long as you can.

What if you don't get your weapon out by the time you get to the grapple stage? Hit, scratch, elbow, spit, bite, kick, gouge, and all the while, try and let the people in the next county know what's going on. Don't

yell *"rape,"* either. The correct word is *"fire."* I don't understand why, but somehow, the word "rape" tells bystanders not to get involved.

ARE YOU A MARTIAL ARTIST?

If you become proficient at martial arts, don't rely on them. Use the DefCon system. To employ most martial arts techniques you have to let the danger get too close before you can work your magic. Even if your magic works, you may suffer some severe destruction during the fracas.

Martial arts techniques, as well as many street fighting techniques—knees to the groin, stomping the vamp of a foot—all require close contact with an enemy who is normally stronger and more willful. Even if you think you're strong, try wrestling with a rapist on drugs.

Don't let any threat escalate to DefCon #3. Handle all rape attempts by long distance. Stay ready to strike. Dress for defense. Wear comfortable clothes you can move around in. Footwear needs to give you maneuverability instead of style.

WHAT TO DO <u>DURING</u> AN ATTACK (SUBMISSION?)

For quite some time, women were advised to submit to a rapist and not resist. That school of thought was probably developed by police departments at a time when officers were mostly male. The submission idea was terrible. Those who committed the crimes were encouraged by submission to do more. Those who submitted added severe guilt to PRTD (Post-Rape-Trauma-Disorder). Finally, legitimate husbands had only to frown at their mates to create even more guilt, as if they had committed adultery. Some husbands even used the incident as justification for their own sexual misadventures.

Now that society has more experience and more study, we know that more than half of attempted rapes can be defeated by a willful woman. A rapist is into a power trip and this is his estimate of power: It's <u>his strength</u> compared to the <u>victim's weakness</u>. If you cry, drop into an emotional fit, go weak and submit, he becomes empowered and it arouses him. On the contrary, if you become powerful, it turns him off.

If the rapist proceeds to a point where there is physical contact between the two of you, **be constantly alert for an opportunity to counter attack while he's distracted.** Look for a weapon. (Anything that lengthens or strengthens your sphere of defense). Got a rat tail comb nearby? I guarantee that inserting it in one ear and driving it out the other will somehow impede orgasm. If you can't penetrate an ear, try driving it through his adam's apple. If he is trying to kiss

If he gets too close you have to use a short range fighting technique. Here the heel of the palm comes straight up.

Once you hook under his chin, keep pushing all the way through. Good speed on contact will create a pain in his neck.

you, could you bite off the end of his nose and spit it in his face? Of course you can fight, scream, bite, kick. When he gets close to you remember to use your body weapons that work at close range such as elbows, knees and the heel of your palm. As preparation at home, examine all of the weapons you have there.

"DON'T MAKE ANY NOISE."

He is going to hurt you whether you make any noise or not. Make all the noise you can. Hopefully, you're not alone in a remote area. So making a lot of noise and screaming for help might cause someone to hear you and respond or at least call the police. Get all the attention you can. Screaming is also a natural way to get your own adrenaline flowing. It disconcerts the attacker, makes you stronger, and helps you overcome fear-induced paralysis. Instead of being weak, submissive, and cooperative, you become a menace; that's a turn-off.

No matter what you do, scream insults at him; call him names. The earlier you attack verbally, the better. Go to war; stay fighting mad during war; conduct all the psychological warfare you can.

From talking with rape crisis centers, we've learned about PTRD. Some victims can't quit washing, others develop jaw pain from involuntarily gnashing their teeth. Some can't sleep nights, others develop night sweats, and many jump at the slightest noise. For others, the disorders are not as severe because they fought hard, even though they lost. The harder you fight during a rape, the easier it will be later to regain your self respect.

WILL HE KILL YOU?

Dare I sit here in the comfort of an office chair and tell you how to react while you're being attacked? But I did the research so I have the benefit of gathering information over a period of time. When you're under attack, you have to make decisions quickly and the key question is, *Will he kill . . .* More appropriately, *will he kill if you resist.* When I consider all the information I've gathered, I doubt it. This is especially true if he threatens you excessively. I believe the rule of the jungle applies: The lion who growls loudest has the least teeth.

Still, you have to decide. The time to think about what you're going to do *during* an attack is *before* the attack. What are you prepared to do? If you can live with being raped, live. You can try all kinds of verbal dodges such as "I have AIDS."

He doesn't want only sex. He wants to **take sex** by power. If someone gives it to him or delivers it for a price, it doesn't arouse. But if he can take it with power---now---that's exciting! Still, you can try. If you can live with failure in the event no verbal ploy provides escape, then live with it. You might very well be in that large group of women who don't report sex crimes.

Some women see rape as a fate worse than death. Also, I've met some women who are deeply Christian and consider death an opportunity to go to judgement where they expect the best. Determine in your own mind what you will do if rape is totally unacceptable. Purpose to put up a battle that the defense minister of Israel would envy.

ACTIVELY DEFENDING YOURSELF

In active defense you repel the attack so you can escape. If you have a weapon, any weapon, this is the time to make it work for you. Any of the standard weapons--pepper gas, stick, rock in a sock or handgun might get you out of trouble.

USING A HANDGUN IN DEFENSE

If you fear for your life, you may shoot. Don't wound. If you do wound or disable with a firearm, he may take you to court or cause you to be charged with a crime.

Because wounding a rapist is such a bad idea, feel free to load special (more expensive) ammo in your handgun for defense. Ask your gun dealer. Most gun store sales persons understand bullets well. Hopefully, this is ammo you'll never use, but if you have to defend yourself, you can't afford to do an inadequate job.

> Think this is a great move? OK---but it's over-rated.
>
> Directed to the groin, it's only directed to a (PP) pain producer. To be effective, you have to connect solidly with nads and crush them against pelvis---all of which requires force and accuracy.

I believe that a majority of female urban residents who live in a major city and follow normal activity patterns face a DefCon #1 problem often. Take charge of each situation long before you go to DefCon #3. The key to success in using a handgun is to get ready to shoot long before being confronted. That's partially because when your hand is on your weapon, your voice takes on a quality easy to recognize. Another reason, you don't decide to act when it's too late.

With your weapon readied, but not displayed, command this threat to buzz off in the meanest voice you own. Let him know you have the ability to shoot. Once you've announced to a would-be attacker that you're not afraid to shoot, and the attacker still doesn't move off, you have real reason to fear for your life. Almost everywhere, mortal fear makes a strong case for shooting in self-defense.

Once you warn your attacker and he continues to advance, no more talking! Shoot! Keep shooting until you're 100% positive the threat has been neutralized. Permanently! Then fire one more round---perhaps at your overstuffed furniture. Later you may be asked in court whether you fired a warning shot. You can answer, "Yes." You are not required to tell anyone that you're warning shot was shot number three.

In addition to firearms, hair pins, nail files, and keys held so they protrude between the fingers of your fist are weapons you should get ready to use the moment you walk into any area in which you suspect trouble might lurk.

Gentlemen: It's your job to go ahead. Emily Post may call it bad manners, but Emily didn't live in modern times. Be the first off and on the elevator to check for---and encounter trouble. Ladies: If your man does encounter trouble, your job is to run away unless you're armed and dangerous.

In the absence of a firearm, don't forget the weapons you have with you at all times. Your teeth, hands, elbows, knees and feet. As soon as you've

> Male packaging can be deceiving. Just because the guy is good looking, don't discount the danger---especially from date rape.

110

gained the upper hand, escape. Bite, kick, elbow the throat, knee the groin, gouge the eyes, or swing something heavy. Inflict pain, lots of pain, then run! If you inflict enough pain a rapist is going to lose the immediate ability, if not the interest, to commit rape. If you're at grapple range, don't forget to bite. Resist with every bit your strength and knowledge, and all of the resources you have at your disposal.

Practically anything can be used as a weapon in desperate circumstances. With a sharp object, you can try and puncture a rapist's armpit, which will disable him quickly. One company offers a totally innocuous appearing hair brush which is, in fact, a molded fiberglass dagger covered by a round styling brush body. An umbrella is also a good weapon.

IN THE KITCHEN?

Your kitchen is an arsenal. Serving forks, kitchen knives, frying pans,

Author is firm advocate of gun control. He says, "Use both hands when shooting!"

The shotgun is the preferred home defense weapon. But a shotgun won't fit in your purse, and the above will shoot right through the material. Warn, grab, and fire.

Note, barrel in illustration is a little too long and allows criminals to grab the gun more easily.

Also, listen to handgun expert and armorer for Kaua'i Police Department Carl Oliver: "Use Glazer rounds, because they don't ricochet as much and therefore are not as likely to wound or kill an innocent person."

A locksmith told me you can sharpen your keys by filing the pointed end flat on the sides and it won't disable their ability to function---as in your ignition.

Remember to back up the ring and key heads in your palm with a handkerchief. No pain.

Incidentally, house keys attached to car keys can be big trouble if you allow valet parking without separating your keys.

sauce pans full of hot soup and rolling pins are all great weapons. Dozens of other disguised weapons are available. Consider each one around your home and how you would use it. Then practice. Swing your frying pan against a tree in your backyard or in the woods on a camping trip. Don't hit with the flat bottom. *On any striking weapon you choose, strike with he narrowest edge.*

KNIVES? NOT FOR WOMEN

For any defense, <u>choose a knife last</u> unless you really know your martial arts moves, are reasonably quick, and possess a real fighting will. Most rapists are repeat offenders and probably have spent time in jail where a whole new set of sub-cultural values were instilled. A confrontation with a knife may be challenge to them; they will at least try to take it away from you. Then you have a problem. To a convict, a knife is a symbol of power and chances are good he'll fight you for it.

<u>REPORT TO AUTHORITIES?</u>

While the laws and methods we have employed with victims (to protect rapists' constitutional rights) have become less oppressive, reporting a rape still is a frightful thing to do. You face a whole series of unpleasant tasks, from gathering evidence, to reliving the experience, to defending your integrity on a witness

Both of these items are commonly found in kitchens. They won't work for you if they're too heavy to swing quickly. Also, striking with the flat surface doesn't do the job so well. The rule: Always cause the sharpest edge to strike and therefore achieve damaging penetration.

stand before an attorney who's job it will be to discredit you.

As bad as the legal process is, not reporting a rape is one reason why it's on the increase. Many rape experts disagree with one another on methods of escape, whether or not to submit, etc., but the one thing everyone definitely agrees on is that every rape and attempted rape should be reported to the police. As it stands, less than 10% are reported. We think that's one reason rapists typically try to degrade their victims so severely; it leaves the victim with nothing more than a deep desire to get the incident out of their mind. Countering that now is a law in many states that says every alleged rape victim is entitled to an advocate during the exam and interview. Advocates are licensed and they help a lot.

Also, experts agree that victims should seek immediate medical attention. As much as I'm sure you want to, don't clean up or change clothes. You've become an inventory of criminal evidence the prosecution will need. Without that evidence, they may be compelled to make a deal more favorable to the rapist.

Call a local rape crisis center. They know their business and they are there to make sure you get all the help you're entitled to. Generally, police detectives, especially females, can refer you. Allow all evidence to be gathered with meticulous detail. We apologize for the attitudes you'll encounter in some male police officers, who perhaps have just lost everything in a divorce, or who've become hardened in their attitude because they've seen so many rapes falsely reported. Incidentally, women who falsely report a rape commit a terrible crime against all other women. Crying "wolf" is one reason true reports don't get the attention they deserve.

> Practice a few times. Throw water from this pan against a tree until you get the feel of it.
> Then when you have a pan full of hot water or soup on the stove, turn the event into a religious affair---and baptize the intruder.

***

The bad news is: almost half the women in the U.S. will be threatened with rape during their lifetime. The good news is: You can be a member of the other---untouchable half.

The illustration on page 101 should help you remember how to control the situation, which I call "Psycho-sexual." See the factors in the box sides which cause either crime or safety? On the right, (where crime occurs) you see shyness, fear and tears. On the left, (safety) you see shrill voice, anger and hatred. These displays of emotion turn the rapist off.

Apply what you've learned here; be perceptive, strong, defiant, maybe even destructive, and thus go through life unscathed.

During interviews, sheriff's investigators and other police detectives have informed me that almost all rapists and sexual abusers of children never stop. Much like criminals on alcohol and narcotics, they're hooked.

My interviews with perpetrators confirm this.

Sexual crimes are not the only plague with which our society contends. Although the compulsion to commit non-sexual crimes is not as strong, recidivism remains high. Thus, burglars will continue to plunder, arsonists will continue to burn, etc.

The basic compulsion to commit crimes is common, and the plague these people dump on society continues unceasingly. It's as if we were at war. The attacks, the expense, the damage never ends.

This is part of an overall solution: When a criminal develops a certain level of criminal "accomplishment," could not a federal judge declare the offender a non-citizen? The loss of citizenship to a declared (by his actions) enemy of America would then set up a criminal for loss of status to sue, and perhaps imprisonment to a contractor in the third world.

Chapter 10

AFTER THE ATTACK

In some jurisdictions, police departments and prosecutors will give you some leeway if they feel you've committed a crime in good faith. Most, however, won't. To them, you're a number. You first appear on the bad side of a figurative ledger under "crimes." They need you to appear on the other side under "caught," and then again under, "prosecuted and won."

Situation: You've just won a rape encounter, either by shooting, smacking, or baptizing an intruder with boiling soup. An extra human body in your presence is either wounded or deceased. The police arrive. Perhaps you hear, "Anything you say can, and will be used against you in a court of law." When they read you these rights, they are not kidding. But there's more. Some police officers have been known to add a few extra words here, some extra evidence there. Worse than that, some officers lie. Therefore: **SAY NOTHING.** Be completely silent. Ask for an attorney. You might think this "say nothing" advice goes only for police. No-no--don't speak a word about the incident to anyone. If you tell a friend in confidence, he or she may be called into court and examined under oath. Talk to the media? I don't think so.

WHY FEED OUR ENEMIES?
Let's make A NEW LAW: If you're convicted of a felony, you get no government welfare, housing allowance, or food stamps. We agree to let you stay in prison until you can learn a trade and prove you can support yourself when you get out.

The ideal situation occurs after you've made a deal of some kind with a criminal attorney (not the guy who wants to draw your will or write your contracts). Criminal law is a specialty. Perhaps your firm has someone with the right kind of experience. In any event, make sure the criminal attorney you plan to call will be available on a 24 hour basis, since most of the attacks against which you have to defend occur in the wee hours.

You get into trouble, you conquer, you call your attorney, and he shows up soon thereafter. (Note here: Don't you call police after it's over; your attorney does that.) He or she answers all the questions, stands by you, and controls the situation.

Many victims who conquered a criminal during an attack make mistakes. So do cops (who shot 41 times in New York and killed an innocent man). Once charged, the expense and psychological trauma of having to deal with our criminal justice system leave permanent scars. Having an attorney on the scene and **SPEAKING NO WORDS** prevents disaster. Police investigators in many locales will write a crime report you won't believe if you talk to them. Don't even discuss the weather.

IF YOU LOST

Report the crime as soon as possible. If there is physical evidence, make sure to preserve it. Sometimes the smallest, insignificant detail* will help police crack the case.

Prosecutors need to know that you will be an excellent witness in court. If that's not the case, they will make a deal much more easily. Therefore, prepare for court as soon as possible. Make notes about everything when the crime is still fresh in your mind.

Hopefully, you'll never be a victim. If it happens however, you'll be either a winner or loser. If you win---be careful---and **silent**.

---

*Insignificant detail, example: Bicycle laying in nearby lawn, visible from crime scene after crime occurred. Detectives canvassed area asking for child who was riding. They discovered 12 yr old (not a neighbor) visitor to grandma's house who had seen the (two male) perpetrators and knew the color, make and year of the car because his uncle had one just like it. Quick arrest.

116

Often after a crime in which several people have been shot, the perpetrator has been described as a loner---"stayed to himself" kind of person. That's true. Loners and misfits do a lot of violence. Gregarious, sociable people don't because the fear of losing social status with peers keeps them in line.

Today, too many teens don't socially interact with friends. Why? Internet, video games and TV are loner activities. Becoming a loner is a big step in deviating from any social norm.

Chapter 11

KEEPING TEENAGERS
SAFE AND SECURE

Right now, houses near good schools are considered good investments because of the huge burst in births. What will this new crop of children be like? Most experts see an oncoming tidal wave of teen violence. Who will be the victims? Other teens.

CAUSES OF THE COMING CRIME WAVE. TEEN INPUT.

The computer term, GIGO describes a computer result which works for teens as well. Garbage in, garbage out has created human monsters. Newborn children are a good source of government income for unwed mothers. Many children never know their fathers. Others feel abandoned after divorce. Still others never receive positive training. The broken home is common. Single parent homes abound.

GOVERNMENT IN ACTION
a. Spends a fortune to repress the supply of drugs.
b. Spends another fortune creating a huge demand for drugs from a welfare-inspired, fatherless teen population.

> ## HOME SCHOOLING?
>
> Send your child to school? He has to try learning in a class full of illegitimates who come from some very tough places. You risk rape, robbery, drugs and perhaps murder. You gain. . . a graduate who can't do math without a calculator, spell without a computer, or read anything difficult----say, like a government regulation.
>
> I see home schooling as our best solution. Even idiot parents who care will turn out a much better educated child than non-caring masters-in-education, bureaucrats. Besides, we have excellent computer programs that handle the technology of learning.

Can we count on our schools? No chance. Like most of our bureaucracies, schools are top heavy with administrators who often create experimental programs to justify their job rather than teach children. All teachers I interviewed during the last 15 years or so have agreed: The peer pressure to stay stupid is an omnipresent and overpowering force.

Although schools are producing dumber children, the work-world demands smarter employees. So with a poor ability to earn, an absence of parents and a lack of nurturing love plus pressure to buy new goods and maintain a decent image, many children are uncertain about their future. Depression is common. The compulsion for kids to try all kinds of escape is seen everywhere.

What legitimate escapes for teens are available? Over 60,000 internet porn sites, television and video games. By the time the average teen graduates high school, he will have enjoyed watching over **15,000 murders** on television. In addition, he has probably practiced shooting people himself on various video games, where the bodies of victims explode into guts and blood on the screen. "Kill more; get a better score." Because families are broken, teens group together, most often according to same ethnicity. Racial tensions abound. A gang "offers" a teen a haven his non-existent family never provided.

Illicit escapes include drugs, sex and alcohol, all of which appear to enable an uncared for, low down, uneducated, no-future child to get away from life for the time being. Once under the influence, drunk or high-on-drugs teens pull off some amazingly inhuman acts. Just under 90% of teen murderers were under the influence at the time they pulled the trigger. For suicides, the figures show three out of four first get loaded, then load the gun.

Is all of the above sufficient doom and gloom? Perhaps, but believe this: The teen world is rough and will get rougher. For either parents or teens, knowledge of the danger is the beginning of good preparation. You've got a lot of trouble to avoid.

NO TRUER WORDS. . . on the subject of child rearing than those from Dr. James Dobson of *FOCUS ON THE FAMILY*. He says:
"Values are not **taught to** the child,
they are **caught by** the child."

THINGS TO AVOID
PASS ON HIGH SCHOOL

Years ago, I would not allow my teenage son or daughter to attend high school. Things were bad then. Now they're worse. In making that decision, I considered the risk vs the gain. What's the risk? Rape, battery, fear, peer pressure to stay stupid, jealousy. Any gain? The catch phrase, "dumbing down" has become popular as a result of our schools' production. Since value systems are caught by the child, what gain is it for my child to be exposed to bureaucratic mediocrity? Those who can---do. Those who can't---teach. Was the risk worth the potential gain? Not even close.

Are there alternatives? Tutors, perhaps once a week. On the internet, www.class.com teaches students all over the world. I like ACE (Accelerated Christian Schools) schools, which worked so well for my first-born son that he can acquire new knowledge like a sponge at age 35. Start early and draw your child into the

---

GOVERNMENT IN ACTION
a. Legislates against prostitution, the trade of sex for money.
b. Legislates for prostitution by paying for the sex teen prostitutes provide---if the girls successfully become pregnant (monthly for 18 years until the child becomes an adult).

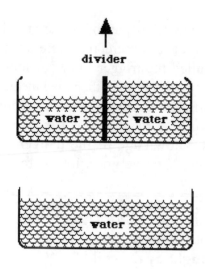

divider

water water

water

PRESSURES IN
PUBLIC SCHOOLS
Families with
teen children need to
realize that they are
like the water on the
right.
Placing your
children in public
school removes the
divider and the water
seeks it's own level.
Result, your
children drop down
in several categories:
Character, learning
ability, health habits,
material things, and
occasionally, life.

pleasure of reading. Biographies of great men and women are essential. I tried to expose my non-schooled children to a variety of licit life styles. Studs Terkel's WORKING for example, gave them an early choice between bricklayer and engineer. You can go to almost any librarian who will help you develop a reading list for your child.

A computer is a necessity. I'm in charge of computer education for my grandchildren. It's cheap. I've paid under $500 for upgraded computers that originally cost well over $5,000. Used children's' educational software can now be obtained (eBay) for roughly $10 per CD. Experts in didactics developed the software. I am told children don't want to stop learning. Mom's get a break. While you have to be careful on the Internet, I've seen lots of good things after I installed my pornography block. The CHRISTIAN CLASSICS ETHEREAL LIBRARY, (www.ccel.org) for example, contains more Christian books than you can read in a lifetime. Large print---works for me.

TERMINATE TELEVISION

I'm finally disgusted with TV content. For a long time, the bad has outweighed the good. My message to the industry: You keep pushing on the sleeze envelope, so sayonara. Even beyond that issue, it's a waste of a teen's time because it allows the teen to absorb without going brain active, which is a key ingredient to thought. TV also lures a child away from social interaction, and the loners are doing some big time damage.

AVOID HIGH FASHION

Don't dress in expensive clothes. Showing off new shoes and clothes invites crime. We've documented stories of dead teens who were shot because they wouldn't give up their expensive shoes or a nice jacket. Other children from different parts of your city might very well have zero respect for you or the things you own. If your child is forced to intermingle with another child who is looking for a way to earn some respect, your expensively dressed, well-mannered child is at risk.

On the other hand, don't wear what other bad guys wear. Pastor Ralph Moore from Oahu once took a troubled nephew into his home and made a rule the kid had to wear denims to school. Gang guys wouldn't talk to him. Drug guys avoided him. He eventually found friends with a "Bible set" and straightened up. Good grades. High moral values. He socialized with girls from a church and eventually joined.

DON'T TEASE

It's real easy to go along with the majority and make jokes about nerds, non-jocks, goths, weird dressers and hot rodders. After Columbine and a few other incidents, I wouldn't recommend sounding off. To a child already psychologically wounded, a cutting remark, sarcasm, or a direct insult may be remembered. The resentment grows and becomes severe. If it creates a desire for real vengeance your child is at risk.

FAILING TO RESOLVE CONFLICT

A grudge held by teens is like a weed in a garden. It grows and chokes out all good things. The Scriptural method is to confront the one who has wronged you. Schools now teach something similar. In today's teen world, inflicting insults, practical jokes, and other kinds of acts which make others feel inferior or angry is not a good idea. Never be confrontational.

PARENTS. BE WARY OF TEEN RAPE

In some areas, 30% of teen girls become pregnant, either by rape or persuasion. The problem: Many boys view rape as nothing more than extra persuasion.

Not only does a daughter have to avoid situations where rape might occur, but she has to be extremely careful whom she dates. Encourage **double dating**. If your daughter spends time alone with a young man, even though innocent, he'll be severely pressured to brag to his friends in a locker room that he did the wild thing---went all the way.

Once that story gets around, she's rapeable. Many teen rapists feel that if the victim did it with others, he's only getting his fair share. Sex with her is a way of bringing himself on a par with his peers. With even a shred of past indecent behavior on her part, she could become an intended victim.

The best prevention here is caring parents who watch carefully the **choice of companions, both male and female.** Listen to Bill Gothard, from Basic Youth Conflicts, "Fathers, you need to interview all of your daughter's prospective dates. They have to learn that you really care about your daughter's well-being. If the father doesn't care and is unconcerned, why wouldn't the boy follow that lead?"

Parents: Spend time with all your daughter's girl friends. Read all emails. Check phone calls. Girl friends who are promiscuous will introduce your daughter to boys who expect sexual favors. While your daughter's companions might put on a great front, look for telltale signs such as provocative dress, foul language, jokes about sex, and rap lyrics. Find out what kind of TV she's watching.

Dig into the family situations of your daughter's friends. A lack of paternal love is poison. When your daughter's friend mentions that "she doesn't have a dad," or, "My father never comes to see me," watch out. Girls without love from a father seek it out—-frequently with older, more experienced males. Of course—-they'll take your daughter along for the ride.

TIPS FOR TEEN SURVIVAL
SELECTING FRIENDS

Be <u>extremely selective</u> about the people with whom you associate. In most cases I have heard about or investigated personally, total destruction occurred because of bad company. Numerous deaths occur because the teen trusted a show-off driver. Most teen drug overdoses happen because the dead victim trusted the dealer. Date rapes ensued after the girl was introduced to the boy by a low character girlfriend of hers.

Be cautious when you meet someone new. If your new acquaintance has EVER been involved with drugs, fathered an illegitimate child, gone to jail for anything, been in trouble with school authorities, showed signs of rebellion, etc. make that person an acquaintance---not a friend. "Hi." end of conversation.

BE CAREFUL AT PARTIES AND DANCES

Much of teen violence occurs at parties because it is an occasion to show off and impress the girls. Fighting is common because boys don't back down when girls are present. Parties are also a time for booze and drugs to be shared. Want AIDS? Share a needle, or get sexually involved with someone who does.

MOM AND DAD ON VACATION?

Remember Karl Malden and, "Don't leave home without them." If you leave teens at home alone, they may have friends over. Could be trouble. We've become a litigious nation. What

---

When I saw my teens in association with others who wore wrong dress, had tatoos, made foul remarks, etc, I got next to that person and dug into character. Bad? I simply told my children he was "off limits." In my daughters' cases, I told the guy as well. Then I enforced my orders.

---

happens if a teen drank your liquor, became totally drunk, and injured someone? Might you be liable? What would happen if someone gets hurt in your home during your absence?

Also, some of the young people who visit your home may rob it on the spot or come back later for more generous portions. How could that happen? Let one teen drug user crash the party— and your house becomes a target because many dealers accept goods for crack, then ship your household goods to another state's swap meet. When they know where to go, kids on drugs can't help but return for more drug-purchasing plunder.

***

For most teens, the peer pressure is overwhelming to stay stupid, get drunk, have sex, and act out rebellion. Often those are the only influences in some teens' lives. Be careful. Avoid evil. Have a full and happy life.

What would have happened had either one of the two shooters at Columbine developed a belief in God?

Not likely though. You know how schools feel about public prayer. A Bible study on campus? Absurd. Yet the Goth movement was free to reign. Where could Harris and Clebold fit in? A sign at the front of the school says, "HOME OF THE REBELS."

After the shootings, the powers considered posting the Ten Commandments. The measure was defeated.

My opinion: Men of proven low character who spend the most (donations from special interests---not bribes) to fool voters get elected and now dictate how and where we worship. Sorry; no chance.

Want a real separation of church and state? If the state can designate a place as a "worship prohibited" area, maybe that same area should be designated "off limits" by the church.

> Child alone on a bicycle alone is often alluring to pedophile who operates in the kidnap mode. They're easy to approach and lure into a car. "I'll bring you back to your bike in just a few minutes if you will help me find my puppy." Riding with others is the safest way to go.

Chapter 12

HOW TO KEEP
ADOLESCENT CHILDREN SECURE

Like Dr Laura, I am my childrens' father. I have four. When my children were young, child abduction hadn't become as prevalent as it is today. Only one thing is worse than experiencing the death of a child. Disappearance. That grieves parents unbearably for the rest of their lives.

ANSWER THE DOOR OR VISIT A LIBRARY ALONE? NO!

CHILDREN: 1. Answer no doorbell rings. Reason: Obvious. Kids are easier to fool than adults, and they make prime hostages. 2. Never visit a public library unsupervised. Reason: Not so obvious. Libraries now show porn on computers over internet, which attracts perverts worse than fruit flies on over-ripe apples.

TELEPHONE PROCEDURES

Children: Don't answer the phone and give any information of any kind to anyone---nothing, nada, zip. Also, don't share any private information with school mates either.

RECOVERING ABDUCTED CHILDREN

Should you fingerprint? I suppose it doesn't do any harm, but I didn't like the idea because it focuses on recovering your child long after the abduction.

This is better because you get them back right away. All the investigation I have done into the crime of child abduction (by a stranger, not a parent) reveals this: It takes a certain amount of time for the abductor to gain the child's confidence.

During that time, you can recover your child or cause the abductor to abandon the crime if you post pictures of your child all over the area. So---why not prepare not only a picture, but a poster that communicates to all the dire urgency of your situation?

Hair up
for photo

Let's start with two pictures of your child for the poster. You need to prepare NOW to make a hundred half-toned pictures within minutes.

Begin by photographing the child twice. Photo #1 needs to be a facial closeup of the child looking confused, angry, or fearful, but **never** smiling. Include any features such as big ears, birthmarks or scars. In addition, long hair needs to be put up in a bun or cut away because perps often cut long blond hair and dye the shorter hair black. So---just the face, please. Photo #2 is of the child standing next to a <u>door knob</u> so everyone who sees a picture of your child gets an immediate sense of height. (Posters declaring your child's height to be 39" communicate zilch).

Now that you have the two photos, have them half toned so they can be copied. Keep master copies with you--- everywhere--- purse, glove compartment, wallet and brief case.

Create a poster called, NEWLY ABDUCTED CHILD !! Answers to the name or nickname of_____. HELP! This little girl was taken at this location:_____. Help me recover my child, and <u>please</u> give any information you have to store security or call 911. Use large **bold** letters so people will be able to read from a distance. Attach both <u>half-toned pictures</u> of the child to the poster and get help in distribution (from security).

Hopefully, the abductor will see your poster before he has created enough confidence with the child to move away from the area. If that happens, he abandons and leaves. When hundreds of people know what your child looks like and the child is still in the area, your chances of recovery are much improved. If your dog is trained, put it on the trail immediately. Should the dog discover the perp hurting the child, it will probably attack.

TRAINING YOUR CHILD IN THE ART OF E&E

My book, *GREAT LIVIN IN GRUBBY TIMES* contains a chapter on Escape and Evasion. It's primarily for military ground troops who might get captured. With child abduction, we're dealing with the capture and loss of 50,000 tiny troops a year and yet, nobody has promoted the idea of teaching children to escape. I think it's more important than teaching ABC's or arithmetic.

Escape and Evasion can be a confidence builder. If ever your child is abducted, hope won't be lost if he or she is well trained in this skill. Make it a game---fun. Play often.

From my military experience as a Green Beret, I know that anyone chasing me will have a difficult time and probably fail if:

1. I can outrun them. 2. I can go places they can't squeeze into. 3. I can get others to help me. 4. They can't see me. 5. They can't hear me. 6. I can neutralize them.

1. Adults (especially those who smoke) are no match for a child who can run several miles without stopping. If your child can run or steal a bicycle, she's safe. Distance creates safety. With a substantial lead in the dark, evasion becomes easier.

2. Normally, kidnappers are large bodied and the child is small and thin. Slipping under cars could keep a grown man from catching a child indefinitely unless there are two people chasing her. Teach your child to analyze the capabilities of men on public transportation. Most abductors are between 28 & 34 years old.

3. Most people in our society are normal and therefore would stop anything, go to any trouble and risk a lot to save a

Teach your child how to destroy a vehicle. Practice with her. Once a car has sugar in the tank, a cut fuel line, missing plug wires, flat tires or a variety of other dis-enablers, her escape becomes a foot race and the perp probably loses.

Also, stealing the license plate, cutting the tail light wires or slicing a brake line will make the car noteworthy to police.

child. Teach your children to print and shout, "**Please. Help me.**"

4. Teach your children about camouflage and darkness. If a child can find a dark shirt to wear and put mud on her shoes and clothing, she becomes much less visible at night. Dirt rubbed into face and the back of hands and arms also help. The one great ally of a child is darkness, but without training, many children are afraid of the dark. Most pedophiles would not expect a night escape and many sleep deeply after drinking alcohol or using drugs.

Start out by going with your little girl into the darkness. Just sit there; listen, observe. Gradually help her overcome fear of the dark and work with her in the escape mode. Games such as <u>Hide and Go Seek</u> are great. Get mom to come and find you.

5. Learn to move silently. This should be easy for kids who wear sneakers. In <u>reel</u> life (Hollywood) you always hear the footsteps of both parties. In <u>real</u> life, once your child becomes silent footed, the pursuer can no longer follow sound. Of course, after she successfully steals the pursuer's shoes she can win easily by running over rocks.

6. Neutralize. Hemlock grows in abundance all over the Southwest. I can't tell you to teach this; use your own judgement. But poison your car? In a minute. Once that's done, your child should have no fear of flagging down a strange car for help.

Perhaps start a fire. Fireman are almost always dedicated to saving children. Once abducted, all hope is not lost if your child has learned to escape and evade!

Your child needs to learn directions! See NEVER GET LOST, the video from Path Finder $19.95. Tap into our: www.**survival-books.com**

Women: **DO NOT** drink alcohol in the presence of strangers. DO NOT leave your drink open and unattended.

Perhaps the newest method for rape involves drink. The guy you meet at a bar buys you a drink and folds a $20 in a certain way that tells the bartender to load it up with GHB or a few other easily made concoctions from commercial chemicals. With those drugs slipped into a woman's tea, soft drink, or alcoholic beverage, she relaxes so severely that she becomes defenseless. Furthermore, she has trouble remembering details. But she was raped---and perhaps impregnated or given a disease.

Chapter 13

DATE RAPES

YOUNG WOMEN: With so much opportunity awaiting you just beyond the horizon, I can well imagine your state of mind. Things are just great. Your school grades are great, several men are responding to your "look," your family loves you, and you are succeeding in a few extra curricular events. Career opportunities abound. Life has progressed nicely, and you are looking forward to an even better future.

Then---WOW---even better, you meet a nice guy and he likes you. He asks you for a date; you accept. During that date, he kisses you and you kiss him back. Sooner or later, the two of you are alone together when you begin to make out with a degree of *passion. His intentions become clear---penetration. You say, "no," but he forces himself on you.

A little afterwards, your future doesn't look so bright; in fact, it took a turn in the opposite direction. You've been degraded. Your self image has crumbled. You may have any number of diseases and one of them might cause death. You might also be pregnant.

If you report the incident, he'll say the sex was consensual and your newly degraded reputation will be published. Will you report this?

---

* Passionate entanglement---your first mistake. As soon as many men are aroused, sexual gratification becomes compulsive. Settle the issue clearly before accepting a date. One man I interviewed wrote a paper about his sexuality stating that it was strong and not to be teased. All women should do the same. Write it once, copy it, and hand it over. Failing that, establish boundaries verbally. If your date pays little attention to the boundaries you establish, he could be a date rapist. Published boundaries are often enough to prevent rape because afterwards, the rapist will have trouble pleading that sex was consensual. Also, he thinks (correctly) that your letter could be entered as evidence to prove no consent---in a trial.

State your reasons for not petting, french kissing or whatever, and then don't give in. A man becomes EXTREMELY aroused when he thinks you made him the special exception to your rules. NEVER do drugs. Be CAREFUL with social alcohol use. You need to be in COMPLETE control of your faculties---and weapons. Furthermore, if you report a rape, it hinders prosecution if he can show you are a heavy drinker etc.

***

Even though many date rapes are not reported, the crime occurs frequently. "He said/she said" makes a poor case to try in court. District attorneys don't want to try a case they can't win.

> You don't have to wade through this chapter if you. . .
>
> ## LEARN A FEW RULES
>
> Double date only until you know your man really well. Never spend time alone unless in a public place. Take alcohol **off** your list of beneficial nutrients. If you must drink, don't let this guy be your designated driver.
>
> The opposite of all the above---date strangers with dinners at either his place or yours. Drink together. Don't set boundaries, and if you do, let him cross those after you've had a few.

If you knew about men as I do, you would be <u>extremely</u> selective about those with whom you socialize and those with whom you go on dates alone. Let me be your guide as if on a museum tour while we examine the macho mind of the male.

We begin with a tour of society around the turn of the century. We were a nation of men and women who built social conduct from Biblical principle. You could do business with a handshake. Doors weren't locked. <u>What were the men like?</u> In the 13th Chapter of Corinthians it reads, "Love does not have bad manners." Most men knew that and therefore were polite. They held women in high regard (level #1 in the illustration). They moved aside for women on the boardwalk. They would hold doors for you, stand to give you the last available seat, care for you and respect you. "Yes ma'am" and "No ma'am" were common expressions. Men who cursed in front of a woman or dis-respected her (Levels #3) were invited to a fist fight. Some were shot. Many rapists (Levels 4 & 5) were hung on sight. Life was physically demanding. Divorce was extremely uncommon. Gradually, those attitudes of respect and awe toward women eroded.

<u>What were the women like?</u> Our first clue: They were--- and wanted to be known as---**ladies.** Today's put-down word, "prude" stands for a woman who is proper in dress, speech and conduct and who does not pass out free sex. The word, "prude" comes from the word, "prudent," which means "judicious or wisely cautious in practical affairs." Today if a woman can be

called a prude, she probably won't wind up pregnant or diseased before marriage. Women of past generations were prudes, great mothers full of Biblical wisdom and prudence who raised sons who respected other women as much as they loved their own mothers. Ladies were well mannered, well spoken and always decently dressed. Most attended church on a regular basis, studied Scripture both alone and in groups and knew quite a few verses by heart. If married, they lived and stayed in submission to a loving husband. They worked hard to provide for their children.

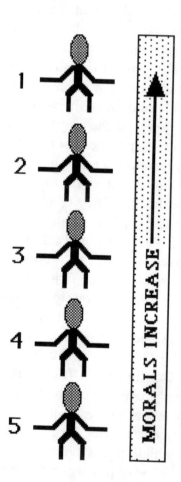

LEVELS OF CHARACTER

#1. Trustworthy. If he says it, it's true. Thinks more highly of others than of self. No gossip. Controls his thoughts and thinks prudently. Self-controlled and secure. Learned genuine love in I Cor 13.

#2. Tries to be genuine. Sometimes fails. Some sexual experiences, but generally adheres to chastity before marriage, in which he probably will be faithful due to self-control. No rebellion in this man.

#3. One of the boys. Desire to belong to peer group caused sexual meanderings. Thinks of some light porn as cool. Allows lower head to make some bad decisions. Leans toward cool things and alcohol.

#4. Too cool to be involved with a woman. Will shack, but plans no marriage. Thinks ugliest word in our language is 4-letter: Half. Belongs to bachelor group. Drinks alcohol fluidly.

#5. Like an Iowa pig, he's been porn fed. Playboy, etc. subscriber. Dresses cool, good dancer, expert at seduction, keeps several girl friends in his stable for security.

Off color remarks by a lady were unheard of. A flash of flesh and public outbursts of anger were un-lady-like and unheard of. Fathers and brothers watched over the weaker sex and often monitored conversations to make sure they were proper. Most young girls had a choice of several eligible bachelors who commonly got down on their knees and pledged their lives---to love, to care for, and support her. Almost all ladies eventually married after which withholding was a word used only by tax collectors. They submitted, and their husbands loved them.

Incidentally, I went to Florida in the late 80's and interviewed quite a few lady widows. They still love their dear departed husbands. They bathed in the good times. They grand mothered families and were surrounded all their lives by love---of a respectful husband, children who honored them, and grandchildren who adored them all over again. To be loved by a child---what a joy. In old age, they became the matriarchs. Cooking for family reunions was always the desire of their heart.

What happened to those men and women of yesteryear? Let me first point a finger at the fair sex. Women wore less in order to be more--- attractive. The make up and cosmetic industry grew. Women altered their bodies to increase appeal. Language loosened. To be popular, women competed in a moral dance of Limbo, "How low can you go?" As in any trend, some young woman pushed at the sides of the social conduct envelope. Men talked about her and she was popular with all the boys. Other women had to

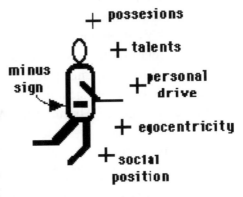

+ possesions
+ talents
minus sign
+ personal drive
+ egocentricity
+ social position

Examine your date. When you discover lots of plus signs, look for the giant negative in self image. Lots of plus signs are almost always compensators for a huge psychological minus.

compete. They wanted to be "in" so they put out. "Making love" in the 50's became the rather impersonal, "having sex" in the years that followed.

What about today? Any art form of a culture reflects the character status of the audience. So you can follow the moral decline of mankind if you listen to the music and watch the Sitcoms. We're growing nastier. . .

Can we blame moral decline on women alone? I DON'T THINK SO! In Romans 2:1, the Bible says, *"Therefore you are without excuse, every man of you who passes judgement, for in that you judge another, you condemn yourself; for you who judge practice the same things."* In other words, when I point a finger at women as the cause of their own ruination, "I have three fingers pointing back at me." (R. Moore, pastor at Hope Chapel, Oahu.) As ladies evolved into loose women, men applauded. We worshiped the creature rather than her Creator. We devised such things as beauty contests, in which WE, men, would judge women based on OUR concept of appeal. We used half-draped women as a lure to sell anything and bought any product endorsed by bosom. Humor which disrespected women became common.

Having sex rather than making love happens when little or no emotional involvement exists. On the other hand, conjugal sex in a faithful relationship is selfless not selfish, and a husband who is commanded by Scripture in Ephesians 5:28 performs in such a way that every bit of physical contact sends a message of love and profound endearment. Absent that emotion, BOTH parties to the act leave with a sense of something missing. That "something missing feeling" gnaws away at one's self image.

People who live together rather than marry make a choice of convenience over commitment. That number has grown to 4.5 million in the United States. Breakups are frequent because they're so easy. Children from those unions know that their days in a happy home may be numbered.

> Just when you didn't think it could get any worse, Hugh Heffner published *PLAY BOY* which included his clever philosophy: Get more. But more was really less if you consider the days and nights when men craved action. Not only that, but the craving intensified. Men (and some women) fed themselves with arousers until they were horny ALL the time. They spent working days thinking about who they could hit on, as well as nights searching, locating, and then exploding in a fit of passion-without-involvement, all of which intensified their horniness soon thereafter.

How does loveless sexual conduct become the norm? Playboys don't want emotional involvement. To love one woman and have sex with another often creates (uncomfortable) guilt. Staying free of emotional involvement appears to provide the freedom for unlimited sexual variety.

"So far---so good," they think. But the recoil in that loveless gun is devastating to the self image. Why? To avoid involvement, they also block out incoming emotions from women. Therefore: <u>Many playboys (levels 5&4) live a life without feeling loved---which deflates the self image.</u> Pornography appears to gratify but actually increases sexual need and lowers image even further.

> ### PROSTITUTE CONTACT. . .
> . . . has to become the death sentence for any man who wants to date a respectable woman. Latent physical disease aside, the mental disease level of a man who has this activity in his history can be dangerous. As a date, you're at risk.
>
> Flesh peddling is the third most profitable enterprise (9 billion) for international criminals. Many women and adolescent girls involved in the trade are **not volunteers**. They are slaves kidnapped from homes and families in foreign lands and tortured, starved and beaten to force compliance, and the "johns" are fully informed because it heightens arousal.
>
> New male friends will often hide a despicable background from you, but will often brag to a fraternity brother or another man at work. Investigate. Network with other women who can find out if anything like this is in a your man's background. Otherwise, you may be dating man who has enjoyed sex with an adolescent slave.

Prostitute contact does the same. It's important for you as a woman to understand this, because this is the process that brings about the search for sexual release and a new self image boost, which is why you became a sexual target.

When a male date has a history of impersonal sexual relationships and perhaps a history of indulgence in pornography, he wants to be a playing boy rather than a loving man. But a lack of love creates a compelling need. Whether it's hunger for food or hunger for love (which the play boy interprets as hunger for sex), deprivation is the mother of severe need. Since most men believe the line between seduction and rape is thin, date rape to satisfy the need as it's perceived is a strong possibility.

Thus we arrive at modern times. We keep making laws protecting women... Although you have a right to say no to sexual advance and only you have legal ownership of your body, date rape now occurs to more than 20% (1 in 5) of dating women.

Look over the men in a modern college student body. Don't they look great? Look again. The majority, over 50%, have admitted to coercion in the pursuit of satisfaction with a date. I call them Darth Vaders (THE FORCE IS ALWAYS WITH YOU). The grey scales in the pie chart are there because we don't have all the data--- because quite a bit of date rape is never reported.

COMPLETE COLLEGE MALE STUDENT POPULATION

How do they go about getting what they are compelled to take? Alcohol is a frequent ploy. Verbal manipulation (guilt) is common. Manipulative anger is another method. A little force is often enough to persuade. Finally, one out of five will force it with brute strength.

Of the one out of five who force it, few get reported. Why? Suppose you're the complainant in a date rape case. These are some of the attitudes commonly found among men. They deny it so strongly you would swear they're running for President. If the DNA is on the dress, (smoking gun proof), they will say it was not only consensual, but you begged for it. If there is evidence of violence, you asked to be handled roughly and things got a little passionate. Furthermore, you were no virgin, so what's one more slice off a cut loaf? Finally, you were a tease and that's what got it started.

During the congressional trial of Clinton for obstruction of justice, the late Judge Higanbotham said, "I've tried 200 cases of car accidents at intersections controlled by traffic lights. In 199 cases, both had a green light." I've tried to interview date rapists. Everyone of them had similar traffic signals on the couch. So I can't tell you what their state of mind is exactly.

Nevertheless, I can warn you about some attitudes you'll see long before your relationship proceeds to that level of destructive intimacy.

His eyes devour you. If you feel undressed by a man's eyes or frightened by the way he looks at you, take heed. Any leering in his visual contact should put you on notice. Also, be cautious with a man who doesn't make much eye contact when he talks to you.

His mouth is out of control. Look for a demeaning comment, especially with reference to your body parts. Double *entendre* is his specialty. If you took it wrong, it's your fault. Maybe it will be a series of off-color remarks about sex. Perhaps he uses bathroom talk. Speech considered by some to be complimentary will make you feel more debased than flattered. Direct address words such as "broad, hot chick, sex kitten, main squeeze," etc, are a clue to his attitude.

His hands roam. It may only be a hand on your arm, but it makes you feel uncomfortable. When a man touches you with caring and emotion, it doesn't feel icky. Generally, when it feels wrong and degrading, something worse is about to happen.

With sexual need up and self image down, **he doesn't relate well.** You can't get rapport with him. You perceive that he's nervous around you and you don't know why. Your sixth sense about this guy gives you a creepy feeling. Something's weird.

Look for signs of a **manipulator.** Does he put you on defense during a conversation? Does he put others down? Is he trying to impress you? If he is the kind of person who makes things happen, you may be the person to whom things happen.

***

Successful dating without rape is principally about prevention, and prevention begins with prudent choice and a clear statement of purpose. Choose well and set the issue straight before you accept a date. When the ground rules are well established with a man of integrity and decent virtue, you keep yourself out of harms way.

I worked as a volunteer for Calvary Chapel's **1-800-Hit-Home** ministry. The main church in San Diego takes calls from teenagers all over the country and routes those calls out to sister churches where the volunteers counsel troubled teens during four hour shifts. My shift was on Wednesdays from 9 P.M. til 0100 A.M. in Arizona.

Our average call-in count: 65. Approximately 72% of the callers were female, and most problems had to do with the results of overactive male libido.

One sixteen year old said, "I'm pregnant and I can't tell my dad." As I saw it, she believed the man when he said "I love you." She dreamed of being loved, accepted, married to her lover. Then when he didn't call in the morning, she knew she'd been deceived.

<u>Fathers! Love your daughters</u> unconditionally. Succeed and your daughter won't be such easy prey for a football hero.

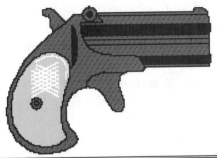

Little guns such as this derringer won't shoot effectively at long range, which limits the gun's use to defense. That's probably a legal benefit. If you use a long barreled .357 and smack a crook a block away, you might have trouble proving you feared for your life.

Chapter 14

FIREARMS FOR PERSONAL DEFENSE

This is the last chapter---because this is the last resort.

How good a bodyguard can you be? You can study edged weapons and become a master of martial arts. You can carry all kinds of whistles and alarms. But in the streets, only one defensive weapon outranks and outperforms all others---that's a firearm.

However, with society's swing against guns and the willingness of enforcement to prosecute any case they can win, using a firearm can get you into more trouble than you could ever believe. Lots of shooters---people of high character---are now long-term residents of a prison.

As with knives, if you draw first, you escalate the problem to the level of lethal. Somebody will die and the other will try, then perhaps fry. If you draw second, you give the other person opportunity to shoot first. So all things considered, shooting a firearm at somebody is a no-win proposition---unless you have to save your life or prevent a drastic trauma to your person such as rape.

Caution! Lack of training makes a gun a liability rather than an asset. Also, if you don't keep your gun secure in storage, some burglar will steal it and trade it for drugs. Then a law enforcement officer may someday ask why your gun recently killed a bank employee.

When you purchase a firearm, you'll probably be introduced to the "rules." For example: "Treat every gun as if it were loaded." Here are a few that deal precisely with your purchase of a gun for protection:

1. On occasion, do you become so angry you go out of control? Don't even visit a gun show.

2. Do you drink alcohol at home while engaging in domestic fights? A loaded gun at home has settled lots of disagreements---permanently. Have **nothing** to do with alcohol or drugs in the same place where a gun is accessible.

3. Never pick up a gun and use it as a threat. It shouldn't be in your hands unless you mean business. If the gun goes off accidentally during an argument, you could become a convict.

4. Do everything you can to avoid serious conflict. Let your dog attack and bite, the alarm go off, or the tear gas spray before you shoot.

5. This is important: **Take no risks.** Never expose yourself to danger. If you like to experience the rush of danger, you're probably better off not to carry a gun. If you ever do find yourself in a gunfight, above all, think **safety.** Break off the engagement as soon as it's safe to do so. The idea is **not** to risk life to save property, and **certainly not** to risk life to get even or defend your honor.

If you absolutely need a weapon to protect yourself and you agree to follow the rules above, disregard the gun control sentiment in this country and acquire a firearm. Learn to use and maintain it, carry it with you everywhere, and practice regularly.

GUN? WHAT KIND?

When it comes to defense, shotguns are best, rifles are second. Handguns are third. That's because of the projectiles they shoot and the accuracy they provide. Rifles and shotguns almost always require two hands to shoot and neither conceals easily. Handguns are most proficiently fired with two hands also, but sometimes you only have one hand available because the other is busy, perhaps driving a car. Even though I recommend you buy a shotgun before any other firearm, and even though rifles will provide long range defense, most gun buyers choose the one-handed firearm option. Therefore, I focus on the handgun, be it automatic or revolver.

HANDGUNS

Choosing a caliber can be confusing, but I can make it simple. Generally, cartridge sizes are measured by diameter. The period you see in front of the number is a decimal point. So, a .25 caliber bullet is one quarter of an inch in diameter, and a .45---almost half an inch. Magnum means extra gun powder pushes the bullet faster. Careful; magnums are harder to control and pose potential danger when they punch through walls on their way to the next city block.

WHAT KIND OF HANDGUN?

Given what we see about guns in the movies, this is an amazing fact but it's true: Most home defense shooting confrontations are settled with one shot. So you need a weapon that works—-every time! You don't generally need a 50 round drum magazine or "the most powerful handgun in the world." You need a weapon you can shoot accurately and effectively under the most stressful circumstances. Therefore, I recommend the double action revolver, which is safe and sure.

For a quick answer applicable to over 80% of gun buyers, this is the caliber to buy: If you're under 5'-10" (145#'s) and of average strength, you purchase a .38 Special, double action revolver with a four- inch (or slightly less) barrel. If you're over 5-10 and strong, consider what we recommend for most males---the same gun-butt in .357 magnum.

What's most important is to make a handgun choice that matches your ability to carry and shoot. If your choice goes bang too loud and recoils too much, you'll flinch when you shoot it and hit very few targets as a result. Also, practice won't be enjoyable when your ears ring and your hand hurts. If your handgun weighs too much, you won't put it in your purse. If you exercise by jogging, the gun must be small enough to fit in the pocket of your sweat pants or jogging suit.

Buy stainless steel unless you enjoy maintenance. It's not that you don't have to keep a stainless clean and lubed. But a blued pistol with sweat on it will turn to rust quickly. After making a choice, outfit your handgun with special, sights, grips that fit your hand and perhaps modify the loading port (if you choose an automatic).

You don't have to shoot the big bang .357 cartridges all the time; you can load it with .38 Specials for practice. But the .357 pushes a .38 caliber projectile about 300 miles an hour faster than the Special. When I wrote *SHOOTING FOREVER,* (all about handguns) my co-author, Dave Smith, cast some bullets with pewter. The .45 caliber bullets were lighter than lead and also harder. Normally .45 auto rounds are slow, but these were fast enough to penetrate an engine block.

Do you need glasses to read? Then don't rely on the original sights; get a different sighting system. Laser red dot sights help make sure you stay on target as you squeeze the trigger. If laser sighting systems are too expensive, purchase a squeeze bottle of glow-in-the-dark Tulip paste and put a line down the top of the barrel (on top of the rib) so you can see your line of fire in the dark. Once you line up the barrel with your target, the only misses you have to worry about will be high or low. (See *EVERYBODY'S OUTDOOR SURVIVAL GUIDE.*)

(WAYS TO CARRY YOUR GUN)

A bare handgun without an easy way to carry it is a burden you'll learn to avoid. That's bad news; you'll wind up with a gun at home when you need it with you. So get good holsters. Built for comfort and easy access, they allow you to carry your weapon

Look ma, one hand. Revolvers are sure fire, no-jammers, so this is best if you don't shoot often. Double action is preferred. The longer the barrel on a pistol, the more accurately it will shoot at a distance. **But,** the easier it will be for somebody close to take it away from you, and the tougher it will be to conceal. Stay just under 4 inches.

with you at all times in a variety of ways. Once you have your holster, modify it. On the straps supporting the holster, hang a few extra rounds in a small pouch, and perhaps a good folding knife which you can open with one hand.

In addition to holsters, you can carry a handgun in a fanny pack, purse or perhaps a surplus tool bag. On the beach or in a park, you can carry a handgun in your towel (see the chapter on travel in this book). Should the need arise, you don't need to draw the weapon because the bullet fires out easily right through the material.

With several methods of carrying, your gun goes with you everywhere; you increase your odds of surviving potential crime attacks dramatically. So---in warm tropical climates, you can use an ankle holster, or perhaps a shoulder holster under your Hawaiian shirt. You can get shoulder holders with vertical, angle and side pulls to provide easy access to your handgun.

What you've read so far provides enough information to make a prudent pistol purchase. Though we could fill a book (and we did in **SHOOTING FOREVER**) let's mention a few others.

Automatic pistols are flatter than revolvers and therefore don't bulge on your body. They also hold more ammo. Many come in a heavier caliber with more stopping power than the .38 Special. But, they're like spouses; automatics require tender loving care if you want them to be faithful. Otherwise, they can fail when you need them most.

Rim fire cartridges are .22's. Someone on drugs may not feel the pain or be bothered much unless you hit a vital organ because the little bullets don't produce knock-down stopping power. If all you have is a .22, the perp will continue to attack if

> Most gun buyers choose the gun first, bullet second, but that's backwards. Choose the caliber first. Find a caliber you can shoot comfortably and well, then buy a gun to fire that size. By the way, don't use round nose bullets like the one shown. They are good for nothing---unless you like ricochets. Think hollow---so your target gets your point.

you don't keep on loading lead into him until the gun is almost empty. (Don't forget to fire a warning shot into the air.)

Since you can't reload a rim fire, you're stuck with the manufacturer's bullet. Penetration through a barricade is inferior and round nose ricochets are dangerous. (Several Los Angeles lawsuits against the city are pending on cases in which a cop shot a bullet which bounced off all kinds of concrete before it wounded a grandmother.)

Choose weapons that provide all the power you can manage, as well as all the weight you are able to carry comfortably. Special ammo adds power and versatility to your handgun. You can buy special cartridges from several special purpose ammo manufacturers. Some really do damage. Also, hot loads are available from Remington, Federal and Winchester.

SHOTGUNS

If you read **GREAT LIVIN IN GRUBBY TIMES,** (found at most Army/Navy stores), you'll pass on a handgun and buy a shotgun for survival. They are cheaper and out-perform a pistol by quite a margin. For home defense, shotguns' big advantages are the power, spread of shot and ability to be fired remotely. Check out my forthcoming book **THE RIFLE RULES.** If you'll be using your shotgun solely for defense, learn to duck-bill the barrel so you'll spread shot sideways.

One decently directed shot from a shotgun will terminate just about any home defense conflict. Anybody who has seen the devastation a shotgun can do at close range has developed healthy respect for this weapon. The thought of a loaded shotgun in the hands of a homeowner causes criminal nightmares.

Like handgun calibers, shotgun shells also come large and small. Ladies get a 20 gauge; men can handle a 12 gauge. The in-between sizes don't make a whole lot of sense. For defense purposes, at ranges less than 20 yards, a load of #2's or #4's from either gauge will do just fine. To be ready for longer range shooting, (+50 yards) go to a double-aught buck load, (designated 00-BUCK on the box) or stay with the rifled slugs that weigh more than most other bullets and travel true to the target because of the rifling around the projectile keep them spinning. These reach out farther than shot loads and provide enough accuracy to be effective up to 100 yards, where they shoot 8" groups.

Don't buy steel shot for defense, especially in moist, tropical climates. Long storage periods in damp climates can cause the shot to rust together, which could damage the shotgun when fired. Shotguns are also called scatter guns, and the farther away you are from a target, the wider the pattern. Of course, too far away and most of the shot may land *around* the target, rather than *on* it. Also, the smaller the shot, (bigger number) the less effective it will be at long range because of wind resistance. That's why some of us prefer slugs.

Pattern your shotgun; it's easy. Otherwise, you'll have to guess where it shoots. Simply shoot carefully at a marked spot on a large cardboard box and see where all the shot goes. You're hoping for an evenly dispersed pattern around your aim point. If your gun doesn't shoot where you aim, either compensate by aiming off or visit your gunsmith.

Criminal interviews reveal that most burglars flee after hearing a shotgun being prepared for battle. But, shotguns require two hands to shoot and can't be carried around easily. They're cumbersome in tight spaces. If you get a shotgun for home defense, folding stocks are a good idea, and laser sighting systems are wonderful for night work.

Don't attach a flashlight to your shotgun. You'll be searching around and while your beam of light is half a dozen feet away from a perp, he'll probably spray lead at the light source.

What kind of shotgun? Do you want an automatic, pump or double barrel? Doubles are fine because they're super reliable. Also, your double gives you an extra quick shot for reinforcement. Like auto pistols, auto scatter guns become temperamental without your TLC. Also a light powdered load in an auto shotgun will cause it to fail while trying to chamber a second shot. Finally, all ammunition doesn't fit all automatics. Attorney Johnny Cochran might say, "If your shells don't fit, you'll be forced to quit."

Pumps require arm action but are more reliable. The tubular magazine under the barrel can hold seven shells. Like an automatic pistol, this is a LIFO loader. Therefore, I put two slugs in first. (To chamber last). In a close quarter squabble, I'll never fire them. That's because tubular magazines on most shotguns provide you with a wonderful facility, you can reload anytime, anywhere, with almost zero down time (time when the weapon can't be fired). You just stuff shells into the tube, either while changing position or hiding safely behind a barricade.

Using a rifle for defense is not a good idea. High power rifles are for shooting long range. Criminals who want to rob and attack you do it from close range.

Understand something very few people consider, probably because of the way Hollywood portrays gunfights. There's a definite hierarchy of weapons, and to stay alive during any gun altercation, you need to respect it. Pistols come in last because they're not effective unless you learn handgun marksmanship, which is not easy. To be a good shot with a pistol requires practice and training. Also, pistol ammo is not effective unless you shoot from close range which is not where you want to be while another handgunner is trying to cancel your ticket. If you plan on using your .38 Special to tangle with someone else using a shotgun or rifle, life insurance would be a good investment.

To survive in any shooting confrontation in which the outcome is decided by hot lead exchange, this general rule applies: **Never risk your life if you have another option. Try to avoid any combat with a weapon where you have only a 50% chance of winning. Break off contact or give up your goods.**

INDOORS. HANDGUN COMBAT

Drawing a pistol in close (grappling range) quarters with your attacker could cause you to lose it. Witness the number of police officers shot with their own gun.

Also, reel life and real life have nothing to do with each other. In Hollywood, the cop enters the room with his weapon held high. Drama. The good guy comes around the corner gun first. Don't do that. Holding high could very well shorten your life span because you'll expose the weapon to a gun grabber. Once that happens, you'll be in a grappling contest with a man--- probably on drugs. Even if you get a chance to shoot, you block your target from your view when you bring the weapon down to fire.

The right way is: Hold the weapon with the sights closest to your eye, which is **down** because the sights are on top! Feel free to fire a round as you bring the handgun up to the hip or eye level position.

The fabled assault rifle. Junk when up against a long distance, high powered shooter like a 7 mm. Remington magnum. Why? High powered rifles shoot long distance accurately, and the M-16 shoots a .223 caliber bullet a short distance at high speed. Result: The assault shooter discloses his location, which enables the long distance sniper to locate him easily in a rifle scope.

My late friend, Marine Corps sniper Carlos Hathcock told me this story as we sat together in his living room. He was in a sniper duel once with a North Vietnamese. Carlos took a shot at a glint of sun off a piece of glass. Later he found out where his bullet had gone---through the sniper's scope and head. The guy was preparing to shoot him--- just as Carlos' bullet arrived.

Carrying an effective weapon on your person will give you a confident attitude. Most criminals read that attitude as a "detour-to-some-other-victim" sign.

Combined with regular shooting practice, a confident physical appearance and quick access to firepower, your chances of winding up in the news as a victim will be substantially less.

***

In closing, this was a difficult book to write. I had to talk with the perps as if I were really in to what they were doing.

Then when I talked to the victims, my heart broke. In a world without "each of us regarding others as more important than ourselves," life is tough---frequently dangerous.

Long range shooter. This is not a weapon for defense. Great survival gun, however. Purchase a caliber you handle with no fear of recoil. Read *THE RIFLE RULES* to become a top pro. Decent shooters routinely launch lead effectively at targets five football fields away.

CONQUER CRIME
Glossary

<u>Automatic</u> pistol. Normally, automatic means hold the trigger down, gun continues to shoot. With handgun, auto means one trigger pull per shot.

<u>Baggie</u>. Usually zip-lock, to hide auto registrations in trunk, and guns under sand.

<u>Case</u>. To inspect and investigate potential theft or burglary victim. Check 'em out.

<u>DefCon</u>. Short for Defense Condition, it's a new system to help you confront danger before it becomes a severe problem.

<u>Germ</u> In this book, a human who infects society by preying on innocent victims.

<u>MACE</u>. Common variety of tear gas spray. New versions add pepper and blind the perp.

<u>Makiwara</u>. Japanese name for short, fist-length, fighting stick.

<u>MP</u>. Military Police person.

<u>Mr Colt</u>. Early pistol inventor. Now it commonly describes a pistol fired in defense.

<u>NAS</u> New American Standard. Version of Bible popular with many because of easy comprehension.

<u>NCIC</u> National Criminal Identification Center

<u>PD</u> Police Department. Normally preceded by other letters, such as M, for Miami PD.

<u>Perp</u>. Short for perpetrator---one who commits crime. Commonly used by police.

<u>Sanctuary</u>. Safe room in your house. Name came first from use of church to secure fugitives from persecution.

<u>Snuff</u>. Real murder of a woman or child in a pornographic movie to increase voyeurs' thrill.

CONQUER *CRIME!*
INDEX
*Chapter headings in **bold** print*

Address for security 27
After the attack 115
    criminal attorneys, pre-visit 116
    importance of silence 116
Airport security, 87
Alliances for safety, forming 88
Armed mugging 10
Assault rifles, worthless 145
Auto registration, hide 56
Awareness about crime 14
Beaches, security measures 94
Bodyguard maxim, great, 6
Bus stations, defenses 87
  Bus travel, dangers 90
Burglary defenses 31
Canes for self defense 65
Carjack-kidnap 50
  Chosen victims, female 51
Carjacking, methods 46
  Defenses 47, 8
  Gas station defenses 55
  Special protection for women 48
  Anti-carjack vehicles 51
Checks, personal, data removed 27
Children, adolescent, security 125
Computer protection 35
Cops choice P-24 64
Dates, checking them out , 5, 74, 133
Date Rape 129
  Rules to prevent 131
  Rapist, signs of 137
Disaster, planning for 43, 44
Display of fear, arousal to rapist 104
Elevators, dangerous 9
Engrave you possessions 16
Escape & Evasion, training for little children 127
Evidence, smallest details for police 116

Flashlights for self-defense 66
Foreign airlines, danger in 83
G. Gordon Liddy, book quote 5
Guns, how to buy 141, 2
      how to carry 143
Handguns for women 18, 139
Handgun in defense 109, 147-8
Hands, bare, for fighting crime 67
Hit from behind, ruse, 49
Hitchhikers, procedures 58
Hostage, choices for you 11
Identity theft 19
   After one dies 21
   Billing cycles, tracking 28
   How it happens 22
   Reducing profile 25
   Victim choice 21
Identity items to protect 20
Items to protect 3
LIFO loading, for men 71
Marriage to foreigner, danger 76
Medical attention, rape victims 113
Pepper Spray 61
  with non-dominant hand 63
Personal Protection 7
Personalized plates, danger in 56
Phone numbers, protect 26
Preparing for crime. 3
Protecting yourself, a necessity 18
Rape by stranger 99
  nature of the crime 100
  rapists' mind set 101
  weapons against 111 et. seq.
Rich? Special precautions 77
  Attack yourself, necessity of 80
  Crimes against, categorized 78
  Matching wealth to caution 77
  Profile to maintain 79
  Protecting against employee suit 80
Riot, planning for 44
Sexual predation 72
Shooting, danger in 34

Signs for Security 36
Singles, crimes against 69
  Women, higher risk 70
Sleeping safely, 86, 7
Social Security number 25
SUV's anti-carjack modifications 52
Taxi, precautions against kidnap 89
Tazers, voltage for criminals 66
Teens, victims of crimes 117
Teen crime causes 117
  drugs as factors in murder 119
  pressure in school 120
Teen crime prevention, don'ts 119, +
Teen survival tips 123
  focus on steady growth 124
Threats during rape, 108
Tipping, dangers in over/under 96
Travel, crime during, 81
  Air travel, precautions in plane 93
  Destinations, crime free 82
  Rules, general for safety 95
  Third world bargains---disaster 83
  Safe destinations 91
  Tokyo and D. C. compared 92
Vacations, leaving teens @ home 124
Vehicle break down, procedures 58
Vehicle, crimes against   45
Vehicle, exits yours @ home 43
Vehicle destruction, teaching children 128
Weapons, non-shooting 59
  Hierarchy 67
Women, anti-rape weapons @ home 112
  Elements of combat   60
  General effectiveness 67

CALL-OUT BOXES

Humor, comments and experiences. Some instruction.

Attorneys, defense tactics, delay, rape 111
Banks, bullet proof walls, danger 16
Bike travel, dangers 87
Bo, experience on TV 64
Convertibles, danger 52

#

Convicts, loss of right to sue 98
Cooperation, law agencies---zero. 17
Credit card, fatal danger in carrying 11, 98
Credit reporting agencies, opt out 29
Criminals and crime, defined 5
DefCon System defines danger 13
Digital cellular phone 40
Dobson, James, Dr, quote on teens 117
DO NOT DISTURB, hotel safety 86
Elbow check for women, weapon? 105
Emily Post, now dangerous 97
Felons, no access to lands 31
Firearms, personal defense 137
Gas station, approach diagram 57
Gun control, support by author 111
Have dinner with a crook? 1
Home schooling, safety in, 118
Mall, carjack pop quiz 55
My failure, burglary 42
Nanny, voice activated recorder use 126
Nicole Simpson, defenseless in Ca 74
Noise traps for home 39
Opting out, form letter 26
Overseas prisons, a real deterrent 6
Paternal love, defense to date rape 101
Pre-nuptial agreements 78
President Carter's illegitimates 3
Purse snatch, second day 11
Residence, choice 32
Robbery, what to do during 10
Shotgun smarts 144
Shoulder surfing 18
Smart government 118, 119
SUV's---anti-carjack 52
Togetherness, anti-carjack 53
Traffic fight, four-wheel escape 54
Travel modes, comparative security 81
Vehicle registration, hide 45
Voice patterns to prevent identity theft 24
Welfare, loss of, for felons 115
Women, cautions, auto repair 48

#